Spelling It Out

How Words Work & How to Teach Them

Revised edition

Spelling can be a source of anxiety for school children and working professionals alike. Yet the spelling of words in English is not as random or chaotic as it is often perceived to be; rather, it is a system based on both meaning and a fascinating linguistic history.

Misty Adoniou's public articles on the processes of teaching and learning spelling have garnered an overwhelming response from concerned parents and teachers looking for effective solutions to the problems they face in teaching English spelling to children. *Spelling It Out* Revised edition aims to ease anxiety and crush the myth that good spelling comes naturally. Good spelling comes from good teaching.

Based on Misty Adoniou's extensive research into spelling learning and instruction, this book encourages children and adults to nurture a curiosity about words, discover their history and, in so doing, understand the logic behind the way they are spelled.

Featuring new illustrations and updated references, *Spelling It Out* Revised edition is an indispensable guide for anyone who lacks confidence in spelling, and an essential resource for parents and teachers of children at all stages of their spelling journey.

Misty Adoniou is Associate Professor in Language and Literacy at the University of Canberra.

T0384618

.

Cambridge University Press acknowledges the Australian Aboriginal and Torres Strait Islander peoples of this nation. We acknowledge the traditional custodians of the lands on which our company is located and where we conduct our business. We pay our respects to ancestors and Elders, past and present. Cambridge University Press is committed to honouring Australian Aboriginal and Torres Strait Islander peoples' unique cultural and spiritual relationships to the land, waters and seas and their rich contribution to society.

Spelling It Out

How Words Work & How to Teach Them

Revised edition

Misty Adoniou

CAMBRIDGE
UNIVERSITY PRESS

University Printing House, Cambridge CB2 8BS, United Kingdom

One Liberty Plaza, 20th Floor, New York, NY 10006, USA

477 Williamstown Road, Port Melbourne, VIC 3207, Australia

314–321, 3rd Floor, Plot 3, Splendor Forum, Jasola District Centre, New Delhi – 110025, India

103 Penang Road, #05–06/07, Visioncrest Commercial, Singapore 238467

Cambridge University Press is part of the University of Cambridge.

It furthers the University's mission by disseminating knowledge in the pursuit of education, learning and research at the highest international levels of excellence.

www.cambridge.org
Information on this title: www.cambridge.org/highereducation/isbn/9781009112871

© Cambridge University Press 2016, 2022

First published 2016
Revised edition 2022

Cover designed by Anne-Marie Reeves
Typeset by Straive
Printed in China by C & C Offset Printing Co., Ltd., December 2021

A catalogue record for this publication is available from the British Library

A catalogue record for this book is available from the National Library of Australia

ISBN 978-1-009-11287-1 Paperback

Contents

Preface

After writing an article titled 'Why some kids can't spell and why spelling tests won't help' for an online news site, I was inundated with emails from parents, teachers and grandparents concerned about the spelling skills of the children in their lives.

Spelling matters, it seems. Even in an age of spell check and autocorrect – spelling matters.

It matters because spelling errors are so visible and open to the judgement of others. It matters because fear of making spelling errors deters many from writing. It matters because there is a strong connection between good spelling and reading comprehension. As educators around the world seek to improve the reading and writing skills of their students, it is important they include spelling instruction in that effort.

Each request I receive for help with spelling is made out of frustration that nothing people have tried so far is working, and each of their stories offers a clue as to why spelling is such a challenge for so many.

The spelling of words in English is not random and chaotic; it's a fascinating treasure hunt that lays bare the history of the language. My responses to the many queries were filled with ideas about how to get children interested in words, curious about why they are spelled the way they are and skilled in discovering their history.

The positioning of spelling as a treasure hunt is not merely an exercise in making spelling 'fun', although it certainly can be. Rather, it is opening up multiple pathways into spelling words that poor spellers simply haven't been given before.

As one reader wrote to me in response to these ideas,

This is fascinating! Honestly I am grinning from ear to ear and giddily skipping about. My husband kind of half

glanced up at me and said 'What's going on?' All I could tell him was that you responded and told me all these incredible things I never knew! My son and I are going to have so much fun discovering words together. Seriously, what a blessing. Now I'm thinking maybe I should have known this study of words existed so I could have majored in that in college ... truly fascinating stuff. It's never too late, right?

She is right. This is fascinating stuff, and it is never too late to learn. The aim of this book is to take interested parents, teachers and carers on that fascinating learning journey.

Acknowledgements

My thanks to all the teachers who have worked with me over the years in research and professional learning workshops. Together we have worked to understand what works best in classrooms to enthuse students and improve their spelling outcomes. Special acknowledgement goes to the teachers of Tasmania, and Weetangera Primary School in Canberra. Their intensive work with me during the writing of this book guided the content and structure of the book so that it would include everything that teachers and parents would find most useful in a book about spelling.

About the author

Misty Adoniou is an Associate Professor in Language and Literacy. She began her career in education as a primary school teacher, teaching in Australia and in Greece before moving into higher education, teaching undergraduate and postgraduate teacher education courses in language and literacy at the University of Canberra in Australia.

She was lead writer for the national English as an Additional Language Teachers Resource for the Australian Curriculum, and has served on several national advisory boards including the Equity and Diversity Advisory Group (advising the Australian Curriculum Assessment and Reporting Authority) and the Orientation Consultative Committee (advising government on the settlement needs of refugees).

She has served as president of two national teachers' associations – TESOL Greece and the Australian Council of TESOL Associations – and on the Board of Directors of TESOL International.

She is the author of many academic and popular articles on the teaching of writing and spelling.

Glossary

abbreviation   a shortened form of a word that has become common usage, e.g. *refrigerator* becomes *fridge*

acronym   a word formed by the initial letters of a group of words, e.g. *laser* from *l*ight *a*mplification by the *s*timulated *e*mission of *r*adiation

affix   an affix is a bound morpheme that is added to the front or end of a base word

base words   base words are usually free morphemes to which bound morphemes are attached

bound morpheme   a morpheme that cannot stand alone as a single word, e.g. *centipede* has two bound morphemes: 'centi' (hundred) and 'pede' (leg)

compound words   two free morphemes joined to make one word

consonant blend   two consonants next to each other representing two distinct 'sounds' (phonemes), e.g. st, sl, br, bl, fr, fl, dr, cl

derivational affixes   affixes that change the meaning of the base word (e.g. adding 'un-' changes the meaning of the base word 'happy') or change the word class of the base word (e.g. adding '-ment' to the base word 'govern' changes the word from a verb to a noun)

digraph   di (two) and graph (symbol) – a grapheme made of two letters representing one sound (phoneme), e.g. consonant digraphs sh, ch, th, ph, ck and vowel digraphs ea, ee, ei, ou, oo, etc.

diphthong   one vowel grapheme that makes two vowel sounds (phonemes), e.g. the 'a' in *cake*, or the 'o' in *go*

eponym   a word named for a place or a person, e.g. *pavlova* for the ballerina Anna Pavlova

etymology   etym (reason) and ology (study of) – the study of the history of words

free morpheme   a morpheme that can stand alone as a single word, e.g. *cupboard* has two free morphemes: 'cup' and 'board'

grapheme   the written representation of a phoneme (sound); it can be a single letter or a group of letters

heterophone   hetero (different) and phone (sound) – words that are written the same but have different pronunciations, e.g. I *wound* the bandage around my *wound*

homonym   homo (same) and nym (name) – words that are written and pronounced the same but have different meanings, e.g. I *left* the highway by taking the first *left* turn

homophone   homo (same) and phone (sound) – words that are pronounced the same but have different meanings, e.g. *cent, scent* and *sent*

inflectional affixes   affixes that change the grammar of the base word, e.g. the verb tense endings 'ed' and 'ing'

morpheme   the smallest meaning unit within a word, e.g. *dogs* has two morphemes: 'dog' and 's'. 's' is a morpheme because it indicates that the base word is plural

morphology   morph (change) and ology (study) – the study of the meaning components within words

morpho-phonemic   how linguists classify a language in which words are spelled according to both their meaningful parts and their sounds, e.g. English

onomatopoeia   onomato (name) and poeia (sounds like) – words that sound like the object or phenomenon being described, e.g. *oink, mumble* or *zoom*

onset and rime   the sound patterns within a syllable. The *onset* is the consonant phoneme or blend at the beginning of the syllable; the *rime* is the remainder of the syllable, e.g. w – in, gr – in

orthography   ortho (correct) and graphy (writing) – a description of the conventions of spelling. For example, drop the final 'e' on the base word before adding 'ing': hide – hiding

phoneme   the smallest unit of sound in a word that can change the word's meaning. For example, the different middle sound in c*a*t, c*o*t and c*u*t changes each word's meaning, hence they are three distinct phonemes in the English language

phonetic   how linguists classify a language in which words are spelled the way they sound, e.g. the Finnish language

phonology   phon (sound) and ology (study of) – the study of the sounds in words

portmanteau   a word made from a blend of parts of other words, e.g. 'smog' from 'smoke' and 'fog'. Note that portmanteaus are not compound words because they are not made from morphemes

prefix   an affix added to the front of a base word

schwa   a very common vowel phoneme that can be represented by each of the vowel graphemes as in wom*a*n, def*i*nite, medi*u*m, small*e*st, harm*o*ny and by more than one letter, e.g. moth*er* and thor*ough*

suffix   an affix added to the end of a base word

syllable   a sound unit organised around a vowel phoneme, e.g. 'win' is one syllable; *window* has two syllables, 'win' and 'dow'. Note that syllables are not morphemes. Syllables break words into sound units, whereas morphemes break words into meaning units

trigraph   tri (three) and graph (symbol) – a grapheme of three letters representing one phoneme, e.g. 'tch' in *watch* or 'eau' in *beautiful*

Chapter 1
Redefining spelling

1

IN THIS INTRODUCTORY CHAPTER, fragments from the spelling stories of children, teachers, parents and carers will be used to paint a broad picture of what spelling is and what it isn't. The following chapters provide more detailed guidance on how to work with children to build their spelling skills in productive ways.

> **Zoe is entering Year 5, and getting very frustrated with herself for still not being able to spell well. I find that she is getting very depressed (even after day 1 of school term 1!) as she is comparing herself to her achieving friends.**

There appears to be a lot of guilt and shame attached to being a poor speller. Many of my responses to the spelling queries I receive begin with 'It's not your fault'. And that seems as good a place as any to begin this book.

Spelling is a learned skill. Our brains are not ready wired for spelling; each individual brain must learn to spell. There are some skills for which the brain comes ready wired – speaking and listening, for example. Reading, writing and spelling, however, have to be learned. How each of us learns these skills will depend, to some extent, on the structure of the brain we were born with, and to a large extent the kind of input we receive.

Because we weren't all born with identical brains, we won't all respond to the same kind of input. So, unless we have some brain damage to specific parts of the brain that deal with language learning, we can all learn to read, write . . . and spell. However, there will be differences in the way we learn these skills. We won't all learn from the same kind of teaching. By and large, problems with learning to spell are a function of the teaching rather than the learner.

Many approaches to spelling instruction reveal an underlying assumption that there is an innateness about a person's ability to spell.

In fact, many of us think spelling ability is something that some of us just have and others don't. And this is a message that is easily passed on to our children, as this mother recounts:

> I am the parent of two children (12-year-old girl and 13-year-old boy) who do well at everything in life except for spelling. They are deflated and constantly tell me: 'Mum, I am just not one of the kids that can spell.'

This kind of 'naturalistic' thinking about spelling is inaccurate and very unhelpful. It leaves struggling spellers with a poor self image that they may carry with them into other areas of their school work and even beyond their schooling years. It also encourages a fatalistic approach to spelling: 'Oh well, we can't be good at everything and spelling is just not your "thing".' As a result some teachers may not bother to investigate the effectiveness of their teaching methods because they perceive spelling to be an innate ability over which they have little influence. They may be less likely to consider the contribution of their own teaching to the issue if they perceive it to be an intractable 'problem' within the student.

The fact that we all learn differently is part of the joy of being human, but it can also make teaching others challenging. Another parent writes:

> I home-school my children. This is my first year. My daughter is a natural speller. It just comes easily to her. As it has, for the most part, to me. My son, 7, however, really struggles. REALLY struggles. And so I've been struggling with how to help him.

Our default position is to teach in the way that we learned most easily and to assume that this will work for everyone. However, teaching everyone the same way doesn't produce the same learning results. Children need to be taught to spell in the way they need to learn, and that may be different from the way their parents or their teachers learned. In her plea, this mother has also repeated the commonly held belief that some people are just 'natural' spellers. In fact, 'natural' spellers are simply receiving the kind of input they need for their brains to learn to spell.

Importantly, spelling ability is not a measure of intelligence, as both research and anecdotes confirm:

> **My son is 8.5 and has autism. He scores in the 95th percentile for comprehension and use of vocab, but in the 5th percentile for spelling. I need to find a way to help him. He's so bad not even the spell checker can sort him out.**

You can have poor spelling skills while being an excellent reader or a creative writer or brilliant scientist. But nor is being a good speller some kind of dumb luck. It isn't simply a matter of having a 'head' for spelling, or possessing an excellent memory.

What is spelling?

If good spelling is simply a matter of good teaching, then it is important to clearly understand what 'spelling' is, in order to teach it.

A simple commonsense definition of spelling is getting the 'right' letters in the 'right' order when you write a word. If in doubt as to what the right letters are, and what the right order is, we can consult a dictionary.

However, words are not simply strings of letters. Words are combinations of letter patterns and meaningful parts. Let's look at an example.

BICYCLE BREAKDOWN

The word *bicycle* is not simply a string of seven letters. It has two distinctly meaningful parts: 'bi' meaning two (consider other bi words like bilingual, bifocal) and 'cycle' meaning circle or wheel. And we can see this meaning structure in the more colloquial name for a bicycle: the two-wheeler. Rather than one string of seven letters to learn, we now have two smaller, and meaning laden, parts to spell.

So how do we know which letters to use when we write those two parts of the word *bicycle*?

'Bi' is a Latin origin word, and it isn't too hard to remember these two letters, which are also fairly predictable letters for the sounds you hear when you say 'bi'. 'Cycle' throws up many more options. Why isn't it 'sikel', for example, as many young writers would probably write? The answer lies in the history of the word, in its original Greek origins *kyklo* – hence the 'y' – and its entry into English through a French filter – hence the 'c's, including the initial 'c' making the 's' sound.

There is nothing natural and intuitive about spelling. The letters that represent the words we speak are the result of a complex history in which humans and their languages have interacted with one another over hundreds of years.

This makes spelling possibly one of the most 'unnatural' of skills we have to learn – which makes it all the more strange that many consider it a natural talent, or something you can simply pick up by taking a list of 10 words home to learn with Mum and Dad for the Friday test. The reasons our words are spelled the way they are have little to do with 'nature' and everything to do with history and society. Every word in English represents a story – a mini lesson in history, geography, linguistics, sociology and politics.

Those who struggle with spelling haven't been taught to look at words this way. They are stuck trying to remember the right order of a string of letters, and that is an impossible task. If words were just strings of letters then none of us could spell. We simply don't have the brain capacity to learn tens of thousands of strings of letters, and recall them every time we write a word. Most of us struggle to remember even one computer password of randomly generated letters. This is because we rely on patterns and meaning to learn anything new, and this is just as true for learning to spell words.

Sounding out?
Heather writes,

> I'm now 28 and for years have been wondering how I could improve in spelling and I am rather self-conscious about it. I listen to sounds and spell what I hear.

As the 'bicycle' example illustrates, English spelling is not a simple exercise in matching sounds to letters, yet sounds-based approaches to teaching spelling predominate in schools.

English sounds and the letters in words have a one-to-one match only about 12 per cent of the time. We have 44 distinct sounds (phonemes) in English but only 26 letters, so letters have to do extra work to represent those additional sounds. Sometimes they do that work by joining together – for example, '*s*' and '*h*' join to make the '*sh*' sound in *sh*ell. Sometimes they do the work in less transparent ways – '*t*' and '*h*' combine to make '*th*'. But 'th' actually makes two of the 44 sounds in English – in *th*is, and the breathier sound in *th*istle.

The 44 sounds (phonemes) of English can be represented by hundreds and hundreds of letter combinations (graphemes). For example, the sound of 'oo' in *moon* can be made by 'o' in *do*, 'ew' in *blew*, 'ue' in *glue*, 'ough' in *through*, 'oux' in *choux* and 'oe' in *shoe*.

In fact there are more than 1200 possible letter combinations to represent those 44 sounds. Compare that to more phonically regular languages like German, a close linguistic relation to English, which also has 26 letters in its alphabet but only 34 distinct sounds, and 39 letter combinations to represent those sounds.

It's this huge variability in English that can cause many people to despair when it comes to spelling. How can we possibly get spelling right when there are so many letter options for the sounds we hear in words? Indeed, the odds of getting the right letters in the right order are very low if sounds are all you are relying on.

More than sounds

English has never been a phonetic language – right from the day 1500 years ago when it imported a foreign alphabet – Latin – as its chosen way to represent the spoken English word in print. Right from the beginning, the letters of the Latin alphabet were insufficient to represent the sounds of the Old English language of the time, and compromises were made, with new letters introduced and old letters given new roles. With phonetic regularity a lost cause from the beginning, English never bothered pursuing it in the ensuing centuries of language borrowing and growth.

English is one of the most polyglot languages on the planet – it has taken words from many other languages. Sometimes those words have come from those who conquered the British Isles, for example, the Norse and then the French. Often those words have come into English as we have looked to the ancient languages of Latin and Greek to give names to new inventions and discoveries. In more recent centuries, new words have come from the languages of those the English conquered or traded with. English words are a reflection of social, geographical and political shifts throughout the history of those who speak English.

As we have imported these words into English, we have often kept the spelling from the original language and applied an English pronunciation to them. And of course there is no single English pronunciation. Ever since English was first spoken, there have been pronunciation differences. In the beginning the differences were from region to region in England, differences that are still clearly discernible today. Then the differences in pronunciation developed from colony to colony – consider, for example, the differences in the accents of the southern states of the United States, Australian English and South African English. Today the pronunciation of English words is incredibly diverse as there are now more non-native English-speakers than mother tongue speakers of English. The sounds of the English words we speak have become ever more distant from the spellings of those words.

All of this means that purely phonics-based – or sounds – approaches to spelling are doomed to failure.

A rich linguistic tapestry

Jean noticed her granddaughter had a spelling problem and writes,

> I used to help her with her spelling list and found that by sounding out the word it seemed to help, but only temporarily as her memory did not seem to be able to retain the correct spelling long term.

If all you have been given as a tool for learning to spell is to 'sound it out', then you have been made a phonological promise that English simply cannot keep. The majority of spelling errors made by poor spellers demonstrate an over-reliance on sounding out. Put simply, sounding out will ensure that you get the spelling of the word wrong, most of the time.

Rather than being a phonetic language, English is categorised as a morpho-phonemic language. This means that a combination of the sound, the history and the meaning of the word influences its spelling. An effective speller draws upon the entire rich linguistic tapestry of a word in order to spell it correctly. The threads of this tapestry can be identified as:

- phonology – the sounds of the word

- morphology – the meaningful parts of the word

- etymology – the history of the word, and

- orthography – the conventions of spelling that have developed over time.

These are interrelated threads. We saw that the spelling of *bicycle* is helped by looking at the morphology of the word: bi – cycle. We also saw that the spelling of 'cycle' is a combination of knowing the phonology of the word and how that is influenced by its etymology (its Greek and Latin roots).

When we understand spelling in this way, spelling is less of a hit-and-miss attempt at a seemingly random and chaotic system, and more an exciting treasure hunt in which each word contains clues to its history and meaning – and the system behind English spelling becomes more evident.

Teaching children to hunt for treasure

The exploration of word histories and meanings is not always evident in classroom spelling instruction. Often, spelling activities involve some kind of rote learning, rather than intellectual investigation, reflecting the belief that words are just strings of letters to be remembered. Often children are asked to learn their words by writing them out many times. Sometimes this is made more fun by asking them to do their lists in rainbow colours or stripes or spirals. When we ask children to learn lists of words by writing them out many times, we are working from an assumption that English has no system – no rhyme nor reason – and that rote learning is the only option. And it is an option that is not helpful to poor spellers.

Marie writes of her daughter's experiences:

Ever since I can remember my daughter has done poorly with the initial spelling pre-test then after a week of rainbow words and phonics activities, gets 100 per cent in the spelling test. She then goes to write a story and the number of spelling errors is still being highlighted. She has learned nothing.

Letter-by-letter memorisation is very difficult; in fact there could scarcely be a more difficult way in which to learn to spell a word. When we do this, we completely strip a word of the system behind it – the very aspects of the word that would make it memorable and logical are taken away, and children are left instead with a string of letters that in most instances bears little resemblance to the sounds they can hear in the word. Spelling becomes a bewildering exercise in memorisation of some very abstract connections between sound and print. Instead we need to show children the stories within words, the linguistic threads that make the system of English much more visible.

All students, but particularly those who are low-achieving spellers, are best served by strategies attached to meaning. These are strategies that allow them to attach their own meaningful stories to words. Storytelling about how words have come to be spelled the way they are, and explicitly teaching the system behind words, helps children to connect the word and its spelling to other information in their brains. This helps them with the spelling of that particular word – and to see the system behind English spelling.

Let's look at the word *yacht* – a word often given in exasperation as an example of how random English spelling is.

Yacht is an imported word from Dutch, *jacht*. You can hear the 'ch' when you say it in Dutch (something like the 'ch' on the end of the word 'loch'). And in Dutch 'j' is pronounced 'y'. So when the word first came into English in the 1600s it would have been pronounced so that you could hear all those letters. Over time, English preferences for pronunciation changed the way we say the word, but the spelling has stayed the same. This is also why we have words like *light* and *night* – we used to pronounce all the letters. Delving deeper into the history of the word reveals a story bound to make it all the more memorable to young spellers. The Dutch origin word *jacht* means 'hunt', and 400 years ago that is the name the Dutch gave to a new type of smaller, faster seacraft they had developed to hunt the pirate ships that were plaguing their international trade at the time. The jet boat of their day!

This brief investigation of the word *yacht* has untangled the phonological (sound), etymological (history) and morphological (meaning) threads of the word. When treated this way, spelling is not only easier but also provides a window to language that supports reading, writing and vocabulary development.

The following chapters contain many examples of how we can teach this way. There are spelling programs that teach children about word origins and the meaningful parts of words. This type of work is usually reserved for the 'advanced' children who have mastered their sounds, but the linguistic threads within words – sounds, meaning, origins and conventions – are neither hierarchical nor strictly developmental. We do not simply move from one to the other as we grow older. All children of all ages benefit from understanding how words work, and all children of all ages are engaged by the stories behind words.

Good spellers draw upon as many sources as possible to get the spelling of a word correct. Spelling bees are a good place to observe good spellers in action. They listen to the word carefully – phonology. They ask for its definition, and to hear it in a sentence – morphology. They ask for its language of origin – etymology. Often they write it on the back of their competitor's sheet as a visual check, and to be sure they are using a plausible pattern of letters – orthography. These are not the strategies of an intellectual elite – just children using every way possible into a word.

If we want our children to be good spellers, we need to give them all the ways into a word. None of us are innately aware of how words work – we need someone to make it visible to us. We need to be taught, and if we are not taught, then who will be a good speller and who will not becomes something of a lucky dip.

The relationship between spelling and school success

Teaching spelling effectively can also support reading and writing development, and vice versa. Understanding how words are made not only improves spelling but also increases children's vocabulary, which in turn improves their comprehension of new words when reading, and enables the use of a broader range of appropriate words in their written compositions.

While spelling is not a measure of intelligence, doing poorly in spelling can affect a child's performance in other areas of school. When children – and adults – feel unsure about their spelling, they can actively avoid tasks that involve writing. And when they do write they often choose phonetically regular words, or words they feel safe with, rather than the words they may want to use. The result can be writing that doesn't do justice to their understanding and creativity.

Spelling programs should therefore be embedded within the whole reading and writing program, and be a part of all encounters with print in all learning areas. For example, unpacking the spelling of the word *polygon* in the mathematics lesson is just as helpful in the learning of the mathematical concept as it is in learning to spell the word correctly. *Poly* is a Greek-origin word meaning 'many', and its Greek origin explains the use of the 'y' instead of 'i' (a lesson we already learned from the word *bicycle*). 'Gon' is another Greek-origin word meaning 'corner'. So the spelling of the word *polygon* also teaches us the mathematical concept of a shape with many corners. This is a lesson we can then transfer to hexa – gon: six corners, penta – gon: five corners. And an aerial view of the US Department of Defense's office makes it clear why it was named the Pentagon.

Spelling shouldn't be an isolated investigation of words for 30 minutes on a Friday morning. When we treat it as such, we run the risk of portraying spelling as a skill we learn simply to perform on spelling tests, and miss the opportunities to use spelling as vocabulary and conceptual development.

Testing spelling isn't teaching spelling

Susannah struggled to see the point of spelling tests for her daughter, recounting:

> **My daughter's school uses the standard spelling methods, and although she does OK in the tests each week, after much painful rote learning, they have no impact on her spelling outside that context.**

With a quarter of a million words in the English language, spelling work is never going to be about learning words by heart. And a weekly test is never going to teach all those words. Even poor spellers spell more words correctly than they ever got right in the ubiquitous Friday morning spelling tests. Spelling tests have little to no influence on our spelling abilities outside the testing context. So it is difficult to understand why they remain so prevalent in so many classrooms.

Probably more than any other school subject, teacher intervention and influence on the spelling abilities of their students is currently negligible. We are far more inclined to test spelling than teach it. When we don't teach spelling, we can take no credit for students' high results in spelling tests, but we bear much of the responsibility for the low results.

Without teaching, it becomes inevitable that the low scorers will continue to score poorly. The children who score 10 out of 10 feel the reward, those who score 3 out of 10 feel the humiliation – again. Often they are sent off to write their incorrect words out 10 times. Little time is given to diagnosing the children's errors, and the process simply repeats itself the next week. Diagnosis of children's spelling errors, rather than simply assigning ticks and crosses to correct and incorrect words, allows us to understand the specific struggles each child is having. This then allows subsequent teaching to address those challenges.

Moving forward

This book has begun by claiming that it is teaching that matters when it comes to spelling success. Good spelling results from good teaching, and teachers need to look forward, rather than to refer to their own experiences, when choosing their teaching strategies. But spelling is much more complex than we might have imagined. You need to know a lot about words to teach spelling well, and it is often a lack of word knowledge that causes teachers, or parents, to shy away from teaching spelling.

Without knowledge of how words work, not only is it difficult to teach spelling but also it means we miss the messages that our children's errors are giving us about their spelling development specifically, and their literacy development more generally.

Chapter 2 focuses on building a knowledge base for each of the 'threads' of the tapestry of words. Chapter 3 provides some principles for teaching spelling based on what the latest research shows us, and chapter 4 gives some practical examples of how to organise a spelling program of your own. Chapter 5 gives some alternatives to the ubiquitous spelling test as a way of understanding what your children's spelling challenges are and to monitor their progress. The appendices provide a range of ready references to lots of interesting spelling facts and resources.

Chapter 2

How do words work? Unravelling the threads

2

Learning objectives

After reading this chapter, you should know:

- how the English language has developed, and how that helps with spelling
- why it is not possible to spell most English words by simply sounding them out
- why spelling rules don't always work but can still be useful
- how English words are made by adding prefixes and suffixes to base words, and why this helps with spelling.

Introduction

HERE'S AN INTERESTING STORY. *Where, what, why, when* and *which* are among the most common words in English. But why do they all start with the 'wh' letter pattern?

In fact, about a thousand years ago these words all began with 'hw' – 'hwer', 'hwat', 'hwy', 'hwen' and 'hwelch'. This spelling was a reflection of their pronunciation, with a guttural 'h' sound before the 'w'. You can still hear traces of this pronunciation in accents in the northern parts of the British Isles. By the year 1200, the people in the British Midlands had dropped the 'h' sound in their pronunciation of these words. They had also become the ruling class. Keen to standardise the English language and the way it was written, because this would make communication and ruling the country easier, they embarked on some spelling reforms. One of those reforms was to spell these 'wh' words the way they were pronounced in the Midlands and not the way those in the north said them. So they dropped the 'h', and for a while we had 'wenne', 'wat' and 'wy'. But eventually it was decided that dropping the 'h' so suddenly may have been a little confusing, so it was popped back in as a visual reminder of the original words. Gone in the pronunciation of most, but not forgotten!

When I tell teachers this story about the 'wh' letter pattern, they are simultaneously impressed and depressed. They are impressed because it is useful knowledge that will remind their students to put in that silent 'h' when spelling the words. They are depressed because they didn't already know the story, and they wonder what else they are unaware of when it comes to English spelling.

It is true that most teachers have limited knowledge of how words work in English. Linguistics hasn't been a feature of their own schooling or their teacher education, and you can't teach what you don't know. The good news is that it isn't hard to build the knowledge – in fact, it's fun. In this chapter we look more closely at the linguistic threads that contribute to the rich tapestry of each word: etymology, orthography, phonology and morphology.

Etymology: Where do our words come from?

The word *etymology* comes from Greek, and it means the 'study of the reason'. Etymology is the answer to *why* a word is spelled like it is. It is most usually explored in the upper grades of primary school or high school. It's often seen as a bit of fun, a sideline dip into the history of words and reserved for the clever kids who need a bit of extension. Indeed, in some popular commercial spelling programs, you can't even look at word origins until you have proved yourself competent at sounds and syllables. But etymology should be the beginning of spelling work with students of all ages and abilities – not the end. If each word is a tapestry, then etymology is the background canvas through which all the other threads run.

To make good use of the etymological clues in our words, we need a basic understanding of the history of the English language.

A brief history of the English language

English is the main language of Great Britain, as well as many current and former British colonies around the world. English is also the most commonly spoken second language in the world. But English is a relatively new language, only about 1500 years old. Compare that to Greek, which is about 5000 years old. As a linguistic youngster, English is a fairly precocious language – it has borrowed a lot from other languages over the centuries. Linguists estimate that about 80 per cent of the words we use in today's English are not 'English', or at least they weren't in the language when it first emerged 1500 years ago.

Old English: The Anglo-Saxons and the Vikings

In 450 AD the British Isles, inhabited by the Celts, were invaded and settled by Germanic-speaking tribes: the Angles, Saxons and Jutes, now usually referred to as the Anglo-Saxons. As conquerors, the Anglo-Saxons were not much interested in the Celtic languages of those they had conquered, and they adopted very few Celtic words into their language. The language the Anglo-Saxons spoke was what we now call Old English, and it would become the English language we speak today.

Old English is impossible for us to read and understand today. Not only was the grammar and vocabulary markedly different, but so was the pronunciation. This was the time when 'what' was pronounced and written 'hwat', and you could hear the 'l' in 'folk' and the 'w' in 'sword'. These are just a few of the words from Old English that are still in our modern English vocabulary. Other words include grammatical function words like *he*, *that* and *to*, as well as everyday vocabulary like *house*, *wife*, *meat*, *drink*, *rain* and *storm*. The surviving Old English words are typically one-syllable words and, although they make up only 20 per cent of the modern English vocabulary, they are among our most frequently used words.

Latin words also found their way into Old English. Some were leftovers from previous encounters with Roman occupations during the age of the Roman Empire several hundred years before. These words were often reminders of the infrastructure the Romans had introduced to the traditional farming tribes they had conquered, for example, *wall, street* and *camp*. But Latin was to have many waves of influence on the English language, and the next big wave came when the pagan Anglo-Saxon conquerors of England converted to Christianity around 550 AD. As

Latin was the language of the Church, many more Latin words entered everyday Old English, for example, *pope, mass* and *candle*.

By the 800s the Anglo-Saxons, who by now were called the English, were unsuccessfully warding off violent Viking invasions from the Scandinavian countries in the north. Eventually the Vikings took over much of the northern British Isles. They spoke Norse, another Germanic language and a close linguistic relative of Old English. New Norse words crept into Old English, for example, *ransack, die, hit* and *ill* – words that might have reflected the less than friendly nature of the occupation. But the most significant influence of Norse on Old English was in the grammar. Verbs and nouns began to lose their complicated endings to indicate person, voice or number, and many of our most common grammatical function words entered the language, for example, the plural pronouns *they, them* and *their*.

Middle English: The Normans

In 1066 the French-speaking Normans successfully invaded Britain. They settled and ruled the country. French became the language of the powerful in Britain, but the powerful kept pretty much to themselves and had little interest in converting the conquered English peasants into French speakers. English was the language of the workers, and French was the language of the rulers. Nonetheless many thousands of French words filtered down into English over several hundred years of French reign. Eventually, the French rulers lost their lands in France and they came to call England home. Before long, they were speaking 'English', the language of the people. But the English language had changed dramatically during this period, and it would have been barely recognisable to the original Anglo-Saxon invaders some 500 years earlier. Old English had developed into what we now call Middle English.

The French words that entered the vocabulary during this period were sometimes brand-new words for concepts, institutions or objects that simply didn't exist before the Norman invasion, for example, *parliament, summons* and *warrant*. But very often the new words already had an English equivalent, like *room* in Old English and *chamber* in French, or *ask* in Old English and *demand* in French, or *pig* in Old English and *porc* in French. So a slightly different meaning was attached to the introduced French word, giving the English language a subtle and nuanced vocabulary. Middle English marked the true beginning of the English language's continuing love affair with words from other languages.

Early Modern English: The Renaissance

By the 1400s the Renaissance had begun. New learning, new expeditions to far-away lands and the advent of the printing press all happened around this time, and each had a major influence on the English language. The printing press made it easier for the printed word to spread, and more people became literate. New words were needed to name new scientific discoveries and ways of thinking, and the English looked to the ancient languages of Greek and Latin for inspiration. Expeditions to foreign lands brought back new and exotic items and a new and exotic vocabulary for naming them. For example, the seventeenth-century explorer William

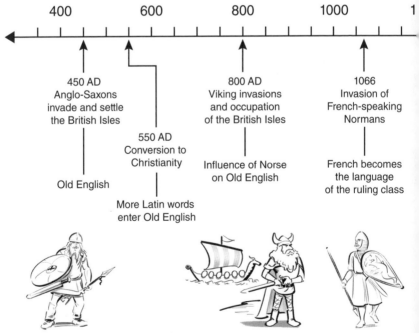

| 400 | 600 | 800 | 1000 | 1 |

450 AD
Anglo-Saxons
invade and settle
the British Isles

550 AD
Conversion to
Christianity

800 AD
Viking invasions
and occupation
of the British Isles

1066
Invasion of
French-speaking
Normans

Influence of Norse
on Old English

French becomes
the language
of the ruling class

Old English

More Latin words
enter Old English

Figure 2.1 A brief history of the English language

Dampier brought back *barbecue* from the Haitians and *avocado* from the Aztecs. Literature and art was flourishing. Shakespeare introduced many new words through his popular plays. Music was enjoying a heyday, and many words came in from Italian, for example, *opera* and *soprano*.

Modern English: The British Empire

By the 1800s the British Empire had spread across the globe, and as English became the language of trade and governance in many diverse countries, words from those countries found their way into English. Such words included *kayak* from the Inuit languages of Canada, *amok* from Malay, *dinghy* from Hindi, *tattoo* from the Polynesian languages and *kangaroo* from the indigenous languages of Australia.

The Renaissance had marked the beginning of what is called Early Modern English, and by the 1800s it had developed into the English we speak today or, at least, something very close to it.

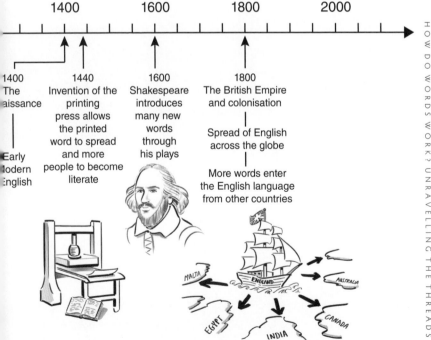

1400 — 1600 — 1800 — 2000

1400
The Renaissance

Early Modern English

1440
Invention of the printing press allows the printed word to spread and more people to become literate

1600
Shakespeare introduces many new words through his plays

1800
The British Empire and colonisation

Spread of English across the globe

More words enter the English language from other countries

MALTA • ENGLAND • AUSTRALIA • EGYPT • INDIA • CANADA

What does history have to do with spelling?

The history of the English language explains much about English spelling. Old English, which had begun as a trio of Germanic dialects, was mostly an oral language. When it was written down, it used a Runic writing system. It was Latin-speaking monks, who had come to convert these Old English speakers to Christianity, who turned Old English into a written language, and to do so they used their Latin alphabet.

A borrowed alphabet

While the Latin alphabet was a reasonable phonetic match for spoken Latin, it was not a good match for spoken Old English. There were sounds in Old English that simply didn't exist in Latin, so there was no Latin letter for them. And there were sounds in Latin that didn't exist in Old English, which left some Latin letters languishing. Those letters were repurposed and some new letters were introduced, but from the very beginning it was a poor phonetic match.

Not only was the Latin alphabet inadequate in capturing the sounds of Old English, but it also couldn't account for the fact that already the pronunciation of Old English differed markedly across the country according to its tribal roots. Every time someone wrote a word, they wrote it according to how it sounded to them, using their best guess at a letter from a Latin alphabet that wasn't really up to the task. The consequence was that spelling differed not only from region to region but also from town to town and individual to individual.

The search for rules

By 850 King Alfred, the first king to successfully unify the various tribes of Britain, decided that a unified approach to spelling would go some way towards keeping his newly allied regions of Britain together. It would improve communications for a start, and he hoped it would increase literacy rates as well. Thus began the first attempt at spelling reform, and there have been various attempts at spelling standardisation throughout the ensuing centuries (in fact, they continue to this day). All are attempts to address the inconvenient truth that English spelling is not phonetic.

By 1200 some spelling conventions had established themselves to stop the practice of simply writing words the way you heard them. Any standardisation of spelling necessarily privileges the speech of one region and one social class – usually the urban upper class of the proposer. In this case it was the pronunciation of the eastern Midlands of England, where the ruling class was located, which guided the spelling reforms. As we learned at the beginning of this chapter, the 'h' was dropped from the beginning of such words as *what, where* and *when*. Some long-vowel sounds were indicated by doubling the vowel letter, for example, *god* became *good*. Other long-vowel sounds were indicated by putting a silent 'e' at the end of the word. Thus *nam* became *name*. Short-vowel sounds were often indicated by doubling the following consonant.

The printing press and the dictionary

The appearance of the printing press brought further standardisation of English spelling, as printers around the country sought to have some uniformity in the way words were spelled in their publications. The first typesetters were not English speakers themselves, and on occasion their own creativity with the language is the cause of modern spelling patterns. For example, they introduced the 'h' into *ghost*, which was a reflection of their own Flemish spelling. 'Ghost' was appearing a lot in their typesetting of the bible, and its many references to the Holy Ghost.

It was a publishing consortium that commissioned the writing of the first comprehensive dictionary of English in 1746. It took Dr Samuel Johnson nine years to complete, but by 1755 we finally had a dictionary of around 43 000 words. Definitions of the words were provided, as well as their use in context and, of course, their spelling. Now printers had a single reference for the spelling of words.

The shift from sounds to meanings

If English spelling had never really been truly phonetic from its beginning as a written language, by the time Dr Johnson had provided that first comprehensive record of standard spellings it was most definitely not phonetic. As many thousands of new words flooded into the English language, attempts to apply an English sound/symbol system to foreign words were abandoned altogether. Both then and today, we have adopted these new words unchanged, embracing their foreign spellings. We treat these words as meanings rather than collections of sounds. English spelling is now well on the way to being the representation of meanings rather than sounds. Modern English has become what the linguists call a morpho-phonemic language; that is, sounds – or phonemes – are one way in which we get our clues for spelling a word, but meaning units – or morphemes – are just as crucial, and perhaps more so.

Etymology is not just ancient history

Etymology is not just about looking back in time. It is about finding reasons for why a word is spelled the way it is. Words come into being not just because they are passed down through time, invasions and conquests. Words come to us in other ways as well. The most common way to coin new words is through joining existing words. We can do this by making compound words where we join two complete words to make a new word, for example, 'moon' and 'light' makes *moonlight*. Alternatively, we can add affixes to a base word. For example, we could add the prefix 'un' to *happy* to make the word *unhappy*, or we could add the suffix 'ness' to make *happiness*. Adding affixes is by far the most common way to make a new word in English.

Portmanteaus

Another way to make a new word is by blending letters of different words to make a new word. These are called portmanteau words, for example, blending 'breakfast' and 'lunch' to make *brunch*. A portmanteau is a travelling bag with two separate components for packing different items. Lewis Carroll, author of *Alice Through the Looking Glass*, first used the term to describe blended words, whereby two meanings could be packed into one word. Carroll himself was keen on making up portmanteau words; *chortle*, a blend of 'chuckle' and 'snort', is one of his inventions. Many newly coined words are examples of portmanteau words, from the more obvious like *scifi*, from *science fiction*, to the less obvious like *modem*, a combination of *mod*ulator and *dem*odulator, and *electrocute*, a blend of *electr*ic and exe*cute*.

Onomatopoeia

Another common source of words is onomatopoeia. Onomatopoeic words sound like the thing they are describing. *Pop* and *zoom* are more obvious examples, but many of our speaking words, such as *giggle*, *murmur*, *whisper* and *shriek*, have onomatopoeic origins. Even words like *laugh* and *cough* have onomatopoeic origins. The final 'gh' in these words was once pronounced, making a sound something like the 'ch' sound on the end of *loch*.

Acronyms and abbreviations

Every now and then we make new words out of acronyms. For example, scuba diving is actually *s*elf *c*ontained *u*nderwater *b*reathing *a*pparatus diving. And LOL began as the acronym for *l*aughing *o*ut *l*oud but is rapidly developing into the word *lol* – a new word for a kind of ironic laughter. Sometimes our new words are simply abbreviations of longer words, for example, *refrigerator* becomes 'fridge', *omnibus* becomes 'bus' and *pantaloons* become 'pants'.

Eponyms

A number of words have their origins in the names of the people or places associated with them. These are called eponyms. A famous example is *sandwich* named after the eighteenth-century Earl of Sandwich, who was so reluctant to leave the gambling table that he ordered his meal be delivered in a manner that would allow him to eat one-handed and still play his round of cards. Perhaps less well known is the macadamia nut, named after the Scotsman John Macadam, a chemist living in Australia in the 1800s.

Why etymology is useful for spelling

Etymology provides the context for understanding the phonological and morphological clues to how a word is spelled. It can tell us why the silent 'h' is there in *what*, and why there is a 'y' in *cycle* and not an 'i'. Etymology can tell us that the 'ian' on the end of *magician* is not a random letter pattern but a meaning unit from Latin that indicates the person who does the 'magic'. Etymology can tell us how different spelling reform attempts through the ages have given us some spelling conventions like the silent 'e', and why these don't apply to more recently introduced foreign words.

Etymology is the starting place for teaching spelling – and not simply an interesting sideline investigation for advanced students. Appendix 1 contains stories of the origins of a selection of words, chosen for the interest they are likely to hold for students, and because they explain why the words are spelled the way they are.

In the next sections we look at the morphological, orthographical and phonological threads of English words.

OUT OF THE BLUE

It is rare for a word to be made up from nowhere at all. Mostly we build our new words on the back of the meanings of other words. Even new technology looks to the past when naming new inventions. 'Phishing', the fraudulent act of trying to obtain people's online pass-words and information, takes its name from the everyday sense of fishing; that is, dangling bait and waiting for it to be taken. But the word in this technological context has been given something of a scientific boost by the use of the classic Greek representation of the 'f' sound with 'ph'. 'Bluetooth' technology, designed to connect different devices, is named for the tenth-century king of Denmark, King Harald Bluetooth, who successfully united the Scandinavian countries of Denmark and Norway.

Question

What is the etymology of these words: portmanteau, onomatopoeia, abbreviation or eponym?

- selfie
- splurge
- panic
- Twitter

Phonology: The sounds of English

Although humans have been speaking for tens of thousand of years, we haven't been writing down our words for that long. Written language began with the Sumerians in Mesopotamia (modern-day Iraq and Syria) about 5000 years ago. But English began to develop its written form only 1500 years ago.

The first alphabets

Writing has always been about conveying meaning. We first began writing down our speech as a matter of convenience and commerce – it was a way of recording business transactions and passing on information.

Our first writing consisted of images to represent the meaning of our spoken words. The cuneiform systems of the Sumerians and Egyptian hieroglyphics are examples. Gradually, because drawings are time-consuming and hard to reproduce the same way every time, they became streamlined – a sort of shorthand for the original drawing. Some of the images or pictograms began to stand for sound units as well, which made it easier to write those things that are hard to represent visually.

Eventually, the Phoenicians got rid of the references to images altogether and invented a writing system in which a symbol represented a sound, giving us the first alphabet. The Greeks used the idea and developed a series of letters that accurately represented the sounds in their language. The Romans followed suit, and developed a Latin alphabet of letters that represented the sounds of their language. That Latin alphabet was used to turn Old English into a written language – and it is also the reason we don't have a neat sound–letter match in English.

English spelling is not phonetic

The Latin alphabet had five vowels, which matched the five vowel sounds of spoken Latin but is woefully inadequate for representing the 20 vowel sounds of spoken English. In fact the most common vowel sound of modern English is the schwa, the sound we can hear in the middle of res*i*dent. And that sound can be represented by each of the vowel letters: a, e, i, o, u, as well as many of the vowel letter combinations. From the time a Latin alphabet was imported to record our spoken English, the quest for phonological consistency was doomed. So we can say English is an alphabetic language because we use combinations of 26 letters to represent meanings on paper. But English is not a phonetic language – our letters don't correlate directly and uniquely with the sounds we make.

Phonemes

The sounds of a language are called its phonemes. Every language has its own set of phonemes, some of which will be unique to it. Phonemes are not any random sounds; they are the sounds that will make a difference to the meaning of a word. So, for example, in English there is a short 'i' vowel sound, as in 'sh*i*p', and a long 'i' vowel sound that we can hear in 'sh*ee*p'. Those are two distinct phonemes in English. However, they are not two distinct phonemes in all languages, and therefore are not sound distinctions that speakers of some other languages need to attend to. English has approximately 44 phonemes. It is not possible to say with complete accuracy how many phonemes there are in English, because it depends upon your accent.

Graphemes

In English, although we have 44 phonemes, we only have 26 letters. The letter or letter combination we use to represent a phoneme is called a grapheme. Sometimes a grapheme can be a single letter. The three graphemes in *cat* are 'c – a – t'. But very often the graphemes have multiple letters. Two letters making a single sound, for example 'sh', 'ch', 'th' and 'ck', are called digraphs. Three letters making a single sound are called trigraphs, for example, tch in *catch*.

We have hundreds of possible graphemes to write our 44 phonemes. For example, we can write the long 'oo' phoneme in *boot* with a multitude of graphemes: 'o' in *who*, 'ue' in *blue*, 'oux' in *choux*, 'oe' in *shoe*, 'ieu' in some pronunciations of *lieutenant*, 'oup' as in *coup*, 'ough' as in *through*, 'ew' as in *brew*, 'ou' as in *soup*, 'u' in *tsunami*. Clearly, unlike the ancient

Phoenicians and Greeks and the modern Finns, we don't spell our words according to the sounds we hear. In fact, there is a simple sound–letter match in only about 12 per cent of words in English.

Phonological mismatches

Sometimes the phonological mismatch is because the words have come from other languages and the letter patterns or graphemes used in those languages are not ones we have classically used in English. Sometimes those letter patterns are representing sounds that we don't even make in English – so we just have our best go at pronouncing them. The 'eau' pattern in *beauty* is just one example of this. It is a French grapheme that represents a French phoneme that doesn't exist in English, and is hard for English speakers both to attend to and to pronounce. So we have kept the French grapheme but applied an English phoneme to it, a sound we can easily hear and reproduce.

The letters in words borrowed from other languages and the English sounds we assign them often bear little relationship to one another. Given that 80 per cent of modern English has been borrowed from other languages, it becomes clear why it just isn't possible to sound out your words in order to spell them correctly.

Accents

Quite often the phonological mismatch has come about simply because English speakers themselves have a wide variety of accents. English pronunciation has changed over the centuries. We once pronounced the silent 'k' in *know* and *knight*. Pronunciation changed, and now it is hard for an English speaker to articulate the 'kn' combination, so the 'k' has been dropped in our pronunciation but it remains in the spelling – to remind us of the history of the word, and to prevent confusion with *now* and *night*.

We tend to keep the original spelling of words even when the pronunciation has changed because, if spelling followed pronunciation changes, we'd be writing new dictionaries every hundred years or so, and there would be a different dictionary for every English accent.

Getting our tongues around words

We like sound combinations that are easy for us to get our tongues around. So we still write 'cupboard', even though we say 'cubbid'. It is just too tiresome for our mouths to pronounce the 'p' when it is being immediately followed by a 'b'. This has to do with the anatomy of our mouths.

The sound 'p' is called a voiceless sound, in contrast to 'b', which is a voiced sound. 'Voiced' means that in order to make the sound, our vocal cords have to vibrate. Touch your throat as you pronounce 'b' and 'p', and you can feel the difference. It is hard to move quickly from non-vibrating to vibrating consonant sounds, so we tend to opt for the voiced one and drop the voiceless one when we pronounce the word. So in *cupboard* we can no longer hear the 'p', but it remains in the spelling. And it is crucial that it does, because without it we lose the meaning of the word.

Sometimes, however, pronunciation wins out and the way we say the word has changed the way we spell the word. For example, the prefix 'in' meaning *not* or *opposite* was applied to *possible*, and the word *inpossible* first appeared in the 1400s. By the 1500s it had become *impossible*, because that was the way everyone was saying it. The phoneme 'n' is formed behind our teeth whereas the phoneme 'p' is formed at the lips. It requires some mouth acrobatics to get from one place to another so quickly when saying the word *inpossible*. In fluid speech our mouths opt for the 'm' rather than the 'n' because 'm' is also formed at the lips, just like 'p'.

But instances of pronunciation leading spelling are not as common as spelling reformers might hope, and that is quite simply because there has never been one pronunciation of English. So although we all see the same letters on the page, we may pronounce them differently. Indeed, as more and more people around the world speak English and bring a greater diversity of pronunciation into the language, the links between letters and sounds become more and more arbitrary. Spelling can be standard, but pronunciation is not. Indeed, you don't need to know your sounds at all in order to spell in English, as evidenced by the tens of thousands of deaf people who spell in English as competently as any hearing person.

How phonology is useful for spelling

This is not to say that phonology is irrelevant to learning to spell. There is a relationship between the sounds of English and the letters we write. See English Appendix 1 in the resources for the English National Curriculum: 'National curriculum in England: English programmes of study' at https://www.gov.uk/government/publications/national-curriculum-in-england-english-programmes-of-study, or the English Language Arts Appendix A for the US Common Core Standards at www.corestandards.org.

But the relationship has become increasingly opaque and in itself is insufficient for spelling a word correctly. Phonology is just one part of the spelling story. If we rely on sounds to spell, we are relying on a phonological promise that English can't keep.

TONGUE-TIED

It's our pesky tongues that are responsible for why we have 'fifth' and not 'fiveth'. The 'th' on the end of our ordinal numbers is voiceless; that is, our vocal cords don't vibrate. But 'v' is voiced. So to make the mouth acrobatics easier, we simply shifted the 'v' to its voiceless partner 'f'. Now we can move easily from the end of 'five' to the beginning of 'th'. And we changed the spelling accordingly.

Question

Through has three graphemes: th – r – ough. How many does *thought* have, and what are they? And how about *cough, enough* and *dough*? What do you notice about the phonemes and graphemes in these words?

Orthography: Getting spelling right

Orthography is the study of correct spelling. Until the production of the first dictionaries, nobody was overly concerned with getting their spelling right. Who was to say what was right, anyway? It was not uncommon to see the same word being spelled in different ways in the one manuscript, and there is a real fluidity in the way words were spelled from year to year until the 1800s. Dr Johnson's 1755 dictionary provided the most comprehensive description of standardised spelling, and for the first time there was a general understanding and expectation of correct spelling.

Spelling reforms and spelling conventions

As recounted in the history of the English language at the beginning of the chapter there were numerous attempts to reform spelling over the centuries because the 'spelling by sound' system was becoming increasingly problematic. Pronunciation in England was different from town to town, and pronunciation was constantly changing. As more and more people became literate, it made sense to have one way of spelling a word to avoid confusion and to make printing and the distribution of the written word more efficient.

The various attempts at spelling reform have given us some spelling conventions that can be applied some of the time when spelling words, for example, the doubling of consonants after short vowels or the dropping of 'e' before adding an 'ing'. However, none of these conventions could be called spelling rules. They are simply a collection of conventions devised at points in time throughout the history of English and, as such, apply most accurately to the words in existence at the time the convention was devised.

As the British Empire grew in the eighteenth and nineteenth centuries, so did the spread of the English language. The pronunciation of words grew even more disparate, and ownership of English language was no longer confined to the inhabitants of Britain. By the 1800s, it was the Americans who were seeking to reform the spelling of English. Noah Webster, father of the American dictionary, had the greatest success. He preferred, for example, *color* to *colour* and *center* to *centre*, and removed the graphemic distinction between the verb 'practise' and the noun 'practice'. Ultimately, these reforms were more about making the point that America was no longer an English outpost and could do what it liked to the English language – more a nationalistic statement than a comprehensive spelling reform.

How orthography is useful for spelling

Orthography is about knowing which graphemes are both plausible, possible and, ultimately, acceptable in English spelling. Although spelling conventions don't apply all of the time, and most particularly not to more recently borrowed foreign words, they are useful. They apply to many of our core vocabulary words, and understanding when and how to apply them helps reduce the hundreds of possible options for spelling a word when relying on phonological knowledge alone. For example, we know that 'ck' is a plausible written representation (grapheme) for the sound (phoneme) 'k' in the middle or the end of a word, as in *chicken* and *duck*. But it is not a possible grapheme for the phoneme 'k' when it occurs at the beginning of words.

Appendix 1 of the resources for the English National Curriculum: 'National curriculum in England: English programmes of study' at https://www.gov.uk/government/publications/national-curriculum-in-england-english-programmes-of-study contains a comprehensive list of spelling conventions.

SKOOL'S OUT!

The spelling of the word *school* is a good example of how fluid English spelling has been over the centuries.

It came into Old English as a word from Latin and was spelled 'scola', but before long had become 'sceole'. The spelling reforms of Middle English meant that 'scole' became the preferred spelling, but by the beginning of the Renaissance we can see 'skule' was in vogue. By 1500 the 'c' had returned and we had 'scule', but another spelling reform in the 1600s popped in an 'h' and 'schole' began to appear. The reason for the 'h' was the Renaissance interest in the classical languages. Although the word had entered Old English via Latin, it was originally a Greek word: *scholeio*. The 'ch' was represented by the Greek letter 'χ' and made the sound we hear on the end of *loch*. Once it had made its appearance, 'h' was here to stay. By the 1700s everyone was writing 'school', and when Dr Johnson recorded it as such in his dictionary, its fate was sealed. School was most definitely in!

Figure 2.2 Spelling 'school'

Question

Spelling reforms have been attempted many times over the centuries. Why have they never been successful? Does English spelling need reforming? What would we lose, and what would we gain?

Morphology: How words make their meaning

Morphology is the study of morphemes in words. *Morphemes* are the parts of the word that carry meaning, for example, *birds* has two morphemes: 'bird' and 's'. 'Bird' is obviously meaningful, but the 's' is meaningful as well, because it tells us that there is more than one bird. Many words are simply one morpheme, for example, *chair* and *table*. But many more words are made from two, three, four or even five morphemes.

Understanding morphemes

Morphemes can be base words or affixes. *Affixes* are the meaningful parts we add on to base words to make new words. When we add them at the beginning of a word, they are called *prefixes* and when we add them to the end of a word they are called *suffixes*.

Compound words

Compound words are two base words joined together. *Chairlift* is a compound of the two morphemes 'chair' and 'lift'. *Tablecloth* is made from the two morphemes 'table' and 'cloth'. With these two examples, the morphemes maintain their original meaning to help us understand the new word. But sometimes the compound word has grown to have a slightly different meaning from its constituent parts. For example, *holiday* has developed from 'holy day'. Holy days were once the days of rest; now holidays are no longer tied to religious days.

Compound words usually start as two words that often collocate; that is, they are often found together in everyday speech. As their relationship gets tighter due to frequent use, the two words become hyphenated. Eventually the hyphen is dispersed with, and we are left with a single word. For example, to-morrow became 'tomorrow', in-stead became 'instead' and e-mail, which was derived from electronic mail, has now become 'email'. When the two words in a compound word are articulated so closely together, the pronunciation of the base morphemes can change, as we saw earlier with 'cupboard'. So while the sounds of the word are no longer the best guide to the spelling of the word, the morphemes are very helpful.

Affixes

Many words are made by joining affixes to base words. There are around 200 affixes in English, about 80 prefixes and around 120 suffixes. Some of these have been in the language since its beginning as Old English, for example '-ness' and '-ly', but most have been borrowed over the centuries from Latin and, to a lesser extent, Greek.

Affixes do different kinds of jobs. Prefixes generally change the meaning of the base word, for example *happy* becomes '*un*happy'. Suffixes usually change the class of the word; that is, suffixes can change the base words into nouns, verbs, adjectives or adverbs. For example, the suffix 'ly' turns the adjective *happy* into the adverb *happily*. Affixes that change either the word class or the meaning of the base word are called derivational affixes. The vast majority of affixes in English are derivational affixes.

Affixes can also tell us something about the grammar of a word, for example in *jumped*, the 'ed' tells us that the jump occurred in the past, and in 'I am *jumping*', the 'ing' tells us the jump is continuous. Affixes that change the grammar of the word are called inflectional affixes, and there are very few of them in modern English, although there were many in Old English.

Affixes do not stand alone – they work with base words to make new words. However, every now and then an affix 'escapes' and becomes its own word, for example the clipping of the prefix off *disrespect* to form the word 'dis' as in 'Don't dis me'.

Base words

Base words can be free or they can be bound. Free base words are easy to recognise as they can stand alone, make sense and be used in a sentence. For example, with the word *sadness*, if we take away the suffix 'ness' we are left with the free base word *sad*. But often base words are bound, and they can be harder to recognise. This means that if you take the affix away, you have a base word that looks a little chopped or unfamiliar, and it cannot stand alone in a sentence. For example, *predict* is made from the prefix 'pre', meaning 'before', and the base word *dict*, meaning 'to speak'. But *dict* is not a stand-alone word; it is a bound morpheme. You can see it working in other words like *dictionary*, *dictate* and *edict*, but it cannot stand alone.

Sometimes the base word has shifted over the centuries from being a free morpheme to becoming a bound morpheme. *Happ* is one such word. *Happ* was an Old English word, a free word meaning luck or chance. Now it is bound, appearing only in the company of affixes, albeit in many of our most common words, for example happy, happen, hapless and perhaps. Appendix 2 contains a list of our most common prefixes and suffixes along with their meanings. It also contains a list of some of our most prolific bound morphemes.

Why morphemes are useful for spelling

Unpacking the morphemes in a word is key to getting the spelling of the word right. Unlike English phonemes, morphemes are quite regular, remaining consistent in their spelling even when phonology changes.

As we have seen with the word *jumped*, if we relied on the sounds we hear, we are likely to spell it 'jumt', but if we think about the morphemes in *jumped*, we find 'jump' and 'ed'. With 'jump' we can now hear the 'p' that had previously disappeared (for much the same reason it disappears in *cupboard*, as discussed earlier), and the morpheme 'ed' is the standard marker of the past for regular verbs. 'Magician' is another example of how an apparently irregular spelling can suddenly become much clearer when the word is unpacked according to its morphemes: 'magic' + 'ian' where 'ian' is the suffix that changes the object (magic) into a person (magician). Very often morphological knowledge steps in when phonological knowledge misleads.

Morphemes are much more useful than syllables as an aid to spelling. Syllables are simply sound units, and breaking words into syllables renders the meanings of words invisible and therefore harder to learn. The two very useful morphemes in 'magician' simply disappear into abstract and unhelpful sound units when the word is broken into syllables: ma – gi – cian.

Understanding how words are built from morphemes improves spelling and increases children's vocabulary. This improves comprehension of new words when reading, and encourages the use of a wide variety of words when writing. But morphological knowledge not only helps you spell the word correctly and improve your vocabulary; it can also teach you about the underlying concept the word represents. For example, 'teen' means add 10, as in six*teen*, and 'ty' means multiply by 10, as in six*ty*. This explains the maths behind the number words as well as helping you spell the word.

Teachers – and commercial spelling programs – are often under the impression that morphological work is too difficult for young children, but morphemes are the meaningful parts of words, and as such they are the most concrete and tangible components of a word. Morphological study should be the foundation of all spelling work with children.

HAVING TROUBLE SPELLING *ACCOMMODATE?*

Understanding the morphemes in a word can help solve some of our most common spelling errors. For example, *accommodate* is made of the morphemes 'ac' – 'com' – 'mod' – 'ate'. 'Ac' is a prefix meaning 'to', 'com' means 'together', 'mod' means 'make fit' and 'ate' is a suffix that makes verbs.

So the double letters are not random letter patterns there to trip us up, but simply the result of joining all the meaningful parts of the word, in much the same way as *bookkeeper*. But in *bookkeeper* the double 'k' doesn't trip us up because we can clearly see the words – free morphemes – that make up the larger word. We understand that one 'k' belongs to book and the other 'k' belongs to keeper. The bound morphemes in accommodate are not so visible to us – ostensibly because nobody has ever pointed them out to us.

- -

Question

What are the morphemes in *forehead* and *breakfast*? How do the morphemes help to understand the meaning of the word, and how do they help with spelling?

- -

Summary

When teachers understand how words work, and why words are spelled the way they are, they are able to teach that knowledge to their students. Spelling is no longer a mystery but a fascinating exploration of words, history and meaning. With strong content knowledge, teachers are able to build their own spelling programs, teaching spelling explicitly as well as taking advantage of teachable moments throughout the school day, encouraging word play and curiosity about the way words make their meaning.

The following chapters explore how to convert this teacher knowledge about words into a teaching program for students.

Chapter 3
How do we learn to spell?

3

Learning objectives

After studying this chapter, you should know:

- meaning is the key to spelling

- spelling needs to be taught explicitly, but in context

- all children benefit from being taught all spelling 'knowledge': phonology, morphology, orthography and etymology

- learning to spell improves performance in other areas of schooling.

A SPELLING TEST

Here is a word for you to learn to spell: *acyanopsia*. Take two minutes now to learn the word, then test yourself. At the end of this chapter you will find out more about the word, and how to learn to spell it.

Introduction

CHAPTER 2 DESCRIBED HOW words work in English, and provided guidance on *what* to teach in spelling. Just as important as knowing *what* to teach is knowing *how* to teach, and that is the focus of this chapter.

Many teachers simply teach spelling the way they were taught – through a list of words to be learned for an end-of-week assessment. However, research shows that this is an ineffective way to learn to spell. This chapter outlines four key principles for teaching spelling, each based on what the research tells us about how we learn to spell.

1 Start with meaning

2 Teach spelling explicitly

3   Teach a repertoire of spelling knowledge

4   Integrate spelling instruction across all subject areas.

Principle 1: Start with meaning

The starting point for all spelling instruction should be learning the meaning of the word. This sounds obvious, but in classrooms all over the country students are learning to spell words they don't know the meaning of. This is curious. How could they use those words in their writing – which is, after all, the point of learning to spell them in the first place – if they don't know what they mean?

Knowing the meaning of a word actually helps you learn to spell it, and knowing how to spell a word helps you learn the meaning of the word. For example, if I know that the meaning of *kilometre* (or *kilometer*) is a unit of measurement for distance, then I might use it in my story writing: 'We travelled hundreds of kilometres on our holidays.'

If I know *kilometre* is made of two morphemes *kilo* and *metre*, and that *kilo* means *one thousand*, I now know exactly the measure of distance represented by a kilometre: one thousand metres. That information is very helpful to me in my mathematics lessons. And knowing the two morphemes in *kilometre* has helped me break a long word of nine letters into two smaller meaningful parts. This will make it easier for me to remember to spell because it eases the load on my working memory (Siegel 2008).

Learning to spell builds vocabulary

When spelling focuses on the meaning of words we also build students' vocabulary, and the size of a student's vocabulary is the best predictor of their success at school. A large vocabulary improves listening and reading comprehension. It also helps students to write with more precision and description.

When learning to spell *kilometre* I learned that *kilo* means one thousand. This helps me understand the meanings of *kilogram*, *kilobyte*, *kilojoule* and *kilowatt*, and being able to break those words into those smaller morphemes helps me spell those words as well.

When we know what the word means but can't remember how to spell it, thinking about the meaning can help us spell it. When we read a word and don't know what it means, unravelling its spelling can help us understand the word. So the two questions that should start every spelling investigation are:

1 WHAT does this word mean?

2 HOW does this word make its meaning?

WHAT IS A JOULE?

Kilojoules are used to measure the energy value of foods. A *kilojoule* is one thousand joules – but what are joules?

Joule is an *eponym* – a word named after a place or person. James Prescott Joule was an English physicist whose work led to the invention of the refrigerator. Joule wasn't the only British scientist to have his name attached to a *kilo*. The Scottish inventor James Watt, most famous for his steam engine, gives his name to the kilowatt. A *watt* is a measurement of electrical power. The average domestic light bulb is 60 watts – so a kilowatt packs a lot of power! Both Joule and Watt had their names immortalised at the very same meeting of the British Association for the Advancement of Science in 1882, where it was agreed to name two units of energy the joule and the watt.

- -

Question

Can you deduce the meaning of each of these words from the spelling? Alternatively, perhaps the meaning of the word helps to spell the word.

- autobiography
- bankrupt
- mistake
- tricycle
- uniform

Principle 2: Teach spelling explicitly

Spelling is a skill we learn, not the natural talent of a lucky few. Chapter 2 demonstrated just how explicable English spelling is, but those explanations are rarely made in the classroom. Most spelling instruction in the classroom reflects the assumption that English spelling is random and therefore unteachable. Very often, spelling programs consist of a list of words provided to the students on Monday, to be learned in preparation for a test on Friday, leaving the task of learning to spell up to the students themselves, or their frustrated parents. The implicit message is that English spelling is irrational and that rote learning is the only option.

We can't learn all our spelling words by heart

We don't learn to spell words by heart. There are around 250 000 words in the English language in relatively common usage, and many of us know close to 60 000 of those words. We didn't learn to spell those words through rote learning. We didn't even learn them in those Friday morning spelling tests, because that would have been 6000 tests, over about 150 years of schooling, assuming we had a perfect score each time.

Learning to spell through rote learning is not only impossible; it is also unnecessarily difficult. When we give students lists of words to be learned by heart, with no meaning attached and no investigation of how those words are constructed, then we are simply assigning them a task equivalent to learning ten random PINs each week. That is not only very hard, it's also pointless. We bring a lot more than our memory to the task of learning to spell.

Too often, when spelling instruction is tackled in the classroom, students are simply given tasks to make rote learning somehow more tolerable – for example, copying the words in different colours, in different shapes and sizes or finding them in word search grids. None of this is helpful in learning to spell, and such activities ignore the fact that there are reasons why words are spelled the way they are.

We spell better when we are taught how to spell

Spelling is something you learn, but not by osmosis. English spelling is a human construction, the result of a complex social history; it is not natural and intuitive so it does need to be taught.

Multiple studies have found that when children are explicitly taught how to spell, they spell better (Bailet 2004, Carlisle 2010, Graham & Santangelo 2014, Henry 1989, O'Sullivan 2000). This is true for all ages and grades – from kindergarten to upper secondary school (Mitchell & Brady 2014). It is important not only to teach spelling explicitly but also to teach it often (Graham & Santangelo 2014). The more spelling instruction children receive, the better their spelling becomes.

Significantly, when spelling instruction is focused on tasks other than preparing for a spelling test, learning from the teaching is maintained. When spelling instruction is focused solely on test-taking, learning is not maintained beyond the spelling test.

Spelling is about learning to comprehend

It shouldn't be a surprise that spelling improves when it is taught. After all, unlike learning to talk, the brain is not ready wired for spelling; each individual brain must learn to spell. Yet even educators whose practices are informed by very different theories of learning still teach spelling in ways that reveal an underlying assumption that there is no structural logic for how words are spelled.

At their extreme, 'whole language' approaches propose that children learn to spell if surrounded by print and that extensive exposure is sufficient to absorb spelling. They promote memory strategies like Look, Cover, Write and Check. This assumes that spelling is simply a visual skill – and that *learning to look* is the key teaching strategy.

At their extreme, 'phonics' approaches disregard the role of meaning in spelling, and propose that the sounds of English are the foundation of spelling. They promote the memorisation of sequences of letters and the sounds they make. This assumes that spelling is simply an aural skill whereby you match sounds to letters – and *learning to hear* is the key teaching strategy.

Although visual checking and *phonology* are components of learning to spell, they are mediated by other information. It is the *etymology* and *morphology* of words that explains the *orthography* and phonology of words. This multifaceted nature of English spelling is not a disadvantage to learning or learners. It is an advantage. The structure of English words means that learning to spell in English means *learning to comprehend*.

Each word represents a meaning, not a sound or an image, and there are multiple ways to approach the word so that both its meaning and its spelling can be understood. However, students will need explicit and accurate instruction to help them gain access to all the information embedded in the spelling of a word.

Q. WHAT DO MAGICIANS AND EDUCATION HAVE IN COMMON?

A. Not much

Explicit teaching of spelling involves more than noticing. Noticing that *magician* ends in the *syllable* 'cian' and *education* ends in the syllable 'tion', and that these two different letter patterns sound the same, does not in itself teach anything about spelling and how words are made.

Syllables are sound-based groups of letters. The syllables of *magician* and *education* are 'ma – gi – cian' and 'ed – u – ca – tion'. When we focus on syllables, both words lose their inherent logic and we miss valuable opportunities to teach about spelling and meaning.

Morphemes are meaning-based groups of letters. As we learned in chapter 2, *magician* is made from the morphemes 'magic' and 'ian', and 'ian' is the suffix that makes the word into the person who does the magic. We can see this suffix at work in *optician, electrician, clinician* and *mathematician*.

Education is made from the morphemes 'educat(e)' and 'ion', and 'ion' is the suffix that turns the verb 'educate' into the noun 'education'. We can see this same suffix in *reaction, action, election* and *direction*.

So, when planning explicit teaching, first we must notice the right things, and then we must teach the meanings and stories behind what we have noticed.

Question

Break each of these words into syllables, and then break them into morphemes. Which are more helpful in learning to spell each word? When are morphemes useful, and when are syllables useful?

- comfortable

- people

- physician

- sister

Principle 3: Teach a repertoire of spelling knowledge

In chapter 2 four linguistic threads were identified as crucial to understanding the spelling of words: etymology, morphology, orthography and phonology. We can call these 'spelling knowledge'.

Many commercial spelling programs deal only with phonological knowledge. A few programs cover all spelling knowledge, but present them as a developmental hierarchy. Students begin with phonological knowledge, learning their sounds and common letter patterns. They then graduate to orthographical knowledge, learning some spelling conventions. Conditional on having moved through these stages, in the middle primary years students may look at morphology, examining common prefixes and suffixes. Finally, advanced students may be encouraged to investigate the etymology of words, particularly Greek and Latin roots.

Research suggests that this is an inaccurate description of how spelling is learned and that the acquisition of such spelling knowledge is not hierarchical but concurrent (Hilte & Reitsma 2011, Kessler & Treiman 2003, Kim, Apel & Al Otaiba 2013, O'Sullivan 2000, Treiman & Bourassa 2000).

This alternative view of spelling development is called a 'repertoire' theory of spelling acquisition (Apel, Masterson & Hart 2004).

Good spellers know a lot about how words work

Children of all ages and abilities can, and do, make use of multiple sources of spelling knowledge when attempting to spell words, particularly when instructed how to do so. Good spellers are differentiated by their consistent use of all spelling knowledge when they attempt to spell words (Daffern 2015). Consider the questions spelling bee contestants ask before attempting to spell a word. They ask for the word's meaning, to hear it in a sentence, and for its language of origin – each of which can provide important orthographical, morphological and etymological information that they can then use as a check against the phonological information they have when they hear the word pronounced.

Brain imaging shows that each spelling knowledge activates different neurological patterns in the brain (Berninger et al. 2010). The more ways you can understand a word, the stronger the 'identity' for that word becomes (Hilte & Reitsma 2011) and a strong word identity is likely to encourage 'generalisation', whereby skills learned in one word can be applied to another (Kohnen, Nickels & Coltheart 2010).

'Sounding out': The phonological promise that English cannot keep

It is true that at different stages of literacy development various spelling knowledge may come to the fore, but never to the exclusion of others.

Phonological work has been shown to have a positive influence on children's spelling in the first two years of schooling. However, phonological skills are only one part of the spelling knowledge repertoire, and a sole focus on the phonological in the early years is not enough to produce good spellers in later years. Instead, it can produce students who become overdependent on the expectation that words are written as they sound. The underlying structure of words remains invisible to them (Henry 1989), and they expect English spelling to stay true to the phonological promise their early instruction has given them.

If students reach Year 3 with no explicit understanding of the ways in which words are constructed, they will fall further behind in their spelling ability, and quite possibly in other areas of literacy that have been shown to correlate with spelling (Carlisle 2010). This is because, by Year 3, around 75 per cent of words students encounter are not phonically regular words. So the 'sounding out' strategy they have been taught in the early years of schooling lets them down for almost every word they attempt to spell. Without a repertoire of spelling knowledge to draw upon, they simply do not have the skills to spell most of the words they need to write.

Morphemes make sense

Morphemes are easy to work with because they are intrinsically meaningful, whereas phonemes are abstract sounds that must be locked together accurately to make a morpheme, from which students must then find meaning. Morphological knowledge is a better predictor of success in spelling than phonological knowledge (Apel et al. 2013, Siegel 2008), and teaching morphological knowledge has been found to improve phonological awareness (Goodwin & Ahn 2010).

Even children in their first year of school can work with morphemes, because they are already morphologically aware in their oral language. We hear them apply their knowledge of *inflectional morphemes* when they say 'I goed to grandma's house', knowing that the suffix 'ed' often marks an event in the past. We hear them use *derivational morphemes* when they call the person who pilots a plane a 'flyer'. This shows awareness of the 'er' suffix indicating a person who 'does' the base verb, and which they have heard in words like *driver* and *worker*.

Delaying work on morphemes until students prove themselves with sounds means that they miss out on years of valuable instruction, and it may also deny them access to the kind of knowledge that may be just what they need to progress in spelling.

A repertoire approach benefits all students – including those who struggle with spelling

Hierarchical developmental approaches to spelling predominate in classrooms. As a consequence many students remain stuck in a developmental stage defined by the program. This inflexible labelling often leaves them without access to spelling knowledge that would be beneficial to them, and with no access to words that are of interest to them.

This is particularly true for low-achieving spellers who are placed in programs that focus primarily on building phonological skills. Many of these students struggle with phonological processing, because of their specific language-learning difficulties. Consequently they find themselves in a spelling Catch 22: unable to achieve in the phonological instruction dictated by the program, and unable to move on to more appropriate instruction because they are not achieving in the phonological instruction.

Without access to the broader underlying structure of words, they lack any other strategies for tackling words. Yet research has conclusively found that, when children with literacy learning difficulties are given morphological instruction, they improve in all areas of literacy, including spelling (Goodwin & Ahn 2010). In fact, it has been found that children with dyslexia improve even more than non-dyslexic children when given morphological training (Siegel 2008). Morphological knowledge provides these learners with a strategy that compensates for their apparent difficulty processing English phonologically.

Children in low socioeconomic status communities, who have traditionally been at risk of low literacy achievement, also benefit from training in morphological awareness (Mitchell & Brady 2014), as do students who are learning English as an Additional Language (EALD). The very different phonemes in different languages make purely phonics-based spelling programs very difficult for EALD learners, who struggle to hear the English sounds, in much the same way a native English speaker struggles to hear the tonal differences in many South-East Asian languages. These students benefit greatly from being shown the underlying system of how words are constructed in English. This not only improves their spelling but also builds their vocabulary and improves their grammar, for example, understanding the job the suffixes 'ed' and 'ing' play in forming verb tenses in English.

If we are not teaching all students the full range of spelling knowledge they can draw upon when spelling words, we are denying them access to tools that would improve not only their spelling but also their achievement in other areas of schooling.

HOW DO YOU SPELL 'DIRECTION'?

When teaching a new word, the first questions should be about meaning, before questions about sounds. Here is a sequence of questions to work through when looking at the spelling of a word. Not all questions apply to all words, but start at question 1 and work through to question 8, using the questions as they apply.

Figure 3.1 How do you spell 'direction'?

Q. 1 Can you tell me what the word means?
The way to go somewhere and how to do something.

Q. 2 MORPHOLOGY Can you tell me HOW it means? Is it made of meaningful parts (morphemes)?
'Direct' is the base word. It is a free morpheme; it can stand alone as an independent word. It's a verb that tells people to what to do or where to go.
    -ion is the suffix. It's a suffix that turns verbs into nouns. So 'direction' is a noun.

Q. 3 ETYMOLOGY Is the word, or any of its morphemes, from another language?
'Direct' and 'ion' are both from Latin.

Q. 4 ORTHOGRAPHY Are there any spelling conventions you know that might help you join the meaningful parts together?
N/A

Q. 5 PHONOLOGY What sounds can you hear as you write each meaningful part?
D-i-r-e-c-t
i-o-n

Q. 6 ETYMOLOGY and ORTHOGRAPHY Does the history of the word or any spelling conventions help you choose the right letter pattern for the sounds you can hear?
N/A

Q. 7 Look at your spelling of the word. Have you seen it written that way?

Figure 3.2 Where have you seen the word written?

Q. 8 Are there other words that have any of the etymological, morphological or orthographical features of this word?

- act – ion

- elect – ion

- select – ion

- -

Question

In chapter 1 we had the story of the spelling of *yacht*, and we have looked at the spelling of *magician*. With that knowledge, work your way through the questions above for each of those words. Which questions apply, and what would the answers be?

- -

Principle 4: Integrate spelling instruction across all subject areas

The main purpose of spelling is to allow us to communicate clearly with others. Spelling words correctly avoids confusion, and it also averts negative judgements of others. Although spelling is not related to intelligence, spelling errors are an easy target for others to snigger at. While correct spelling aids communication and prevents sniggering, spelling instruction achieves much more than this.

Learning to spell improves learning in other areas of schooling

When spelling instruction is focused on meaning, and how words make their meaning, reading comprehension, writing and vocabulary improve, as well as spelling (Apel 2014, Berninger et al. 2010, Goodwin & Ahn 2010, Graham & Santangelo 2014). These benefits are then evident in all curriculum areas (Bryant, Nunes & Barros 2014).

Students who can decode single words when reading but who struggle with reading comprehension have been found to have poor morphological awareness compared to their peers with normal reading comprehension (Apel et al. 2013). Students' morphological knowledge predicts success in reading more effectively than their phonological knowledge, particularly over the long term (Pittas & Nunes 2014). As we have seen, morphology enables students to deduce the meaning of a word by unpacking its components, which gives them information to use when comprehending text.

Informed spelling instruction not only improves vocabulary and reading comprehension but also helps teach underlying concepts. For example, when teaching the concept of *perimeter* in mathematics the teacher can unpack the two morphemes *peri*, meaning 'around', and *meter*, meaning 'to measure'. This helps students spell the word and teaches them that 'perimeter' means they must measure *around* the shape. This clearly differentiates the mathematical concept of *perimeter* from *area* – two concepts students often confuse.

Teach knowledge, not words

There are more than a quarter of a million words in the English language. It is impossible to teach the spelling of every word, so which words should we teach?

The words we choose to teach for spelling are less important than the way we teach them. The focus of spelling instruction should be on the development of spelling knowledge that students can then apply to new words as they encounter them. Nonetheless, we do need to teach this knowledge through words, so when choosing those words we should focus on the words the students *want* to know and the words they *need* to know.

Frequent words

Despite the large number of words in the English language, a significant proportion of those words are made using a relatively small number of affixes. Knowing those affixes is an efficient way to learn to spell many words. Appendix 2 contains a list of the most common affixes and base words.

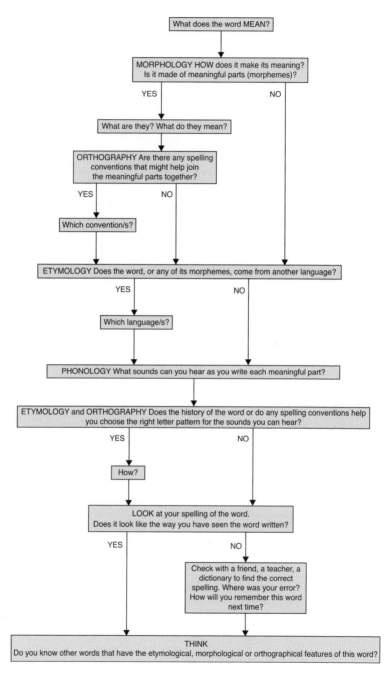

Figure 3.3 Word investigation

The hundred most frequently occurring words in English are mostly our original Old English words, and they are generally single morphemes – words like *what, said, of.* They don't have affixes to unpack, but they do have etymological, phonological and orthographical stories that can help explain their spelling. They also make up 50 per cent of all words in texts, making them a good choice for spelling instruction. Fortunately their prevalence means these words are everywhere and do not need to be learned by heart or in spelling lists. They will be found in all the books children love to read – children's literature and information books – as well as in all the texts they come across at school, from instructions on maths worksheets to the signs around the school.

Useful words

Other words to examine for spelling should come from the topics being studied at school, in all learning areas, and from the words the students wish to use for their own writing. Words could come from the maths textbook, the class novel, the history website, the science lab report and the art gallery information labels. By working with these words students have the opportunity to practise them as they use the words for the real and everyday purpose of communicating with others.

Appendix 3 contains examples of how to approach some of the most frequently used words in English, commonly misspelled words in student writing, and some examples of words that illustrate spelling features most commonly assessed in standardised tests of spelling.

Teach spelling every day, throughout the day

In order to improve our spelling we need to be taught it regularly and repeatedly. Repetition does not mean rote learning. It means we need to investigate how words work, while they are doing their work, and whenever they are doing their work. And words do their work while doing the real job of communicating.

Words do nothing and mean nothing when they sit as a numbered list on a spelling test. When spelling words are learned from an isolated list, they are learned as a discrete skill and quickly forgotten. Let's take our earlier example of learning to spell *perimeter*. It makes much more sense to learn about the spelling of *perimeter* while measuring around shapes in a mathematics lesson than it does to learn it on a spelling list of words chosen because they all share the letter pattern of 'er'.

Growth in spelling expertise through the grades has been shown to be attributable to the students' experiences with authentic texts, rather than words on weekly spelling lists (Treiman & Bourassa 2000). Therefore the separation of spelling from all other learning is of no help to students making normal progress in literacy, and it has been found to exacerbate the difficulties that struggling children have (Bailet 2004).

Summary

Spelling isn't an innate talent. English spelling is not natural, something we can just pick up through exposure. Nor is English spelling a matter of simply matching sounds to letters. The spelling of English words is a complex social construction, which has evolved over time and been influenced by other languages. As such we need instruction from others to help us understand that history and uncover the underlying structures of words. This cannot be achieved by leaving the task of learning to spell up to parents and children through the distribution of take-home spelling lists that they must figure out for themselves.

Students of all abilities benefit when they can draw upon a broad repertoire of strategies to spell words. All students should receive instruction in the entire repertoire of spelling knowledge. Low-achieving spellers should not be left wallowing in phonics programs for years when their lack of achievement in those programs is a clear indication they need a different approach. When we don't teach spelling in meaningful and effective ways, we further disadvantage students, because spelling instruction improves their learning in all other areas of schooling.

This chapter has provided four key research-based principles for the effective teaching of spelling. In chapter 4 we look at how these principles might convert into a classroom program for spelling.

SOLUTION TO ACYANOPSIA

How did you go with the word *acyanopsia*? Did you spell it correctly? Do you think you will remember how to spell it in a few weeks' time? Of course you are highly unlikely to use this word, because you probably don't know what it means – you possibly don't even know how to say it.

Our experience learning to spell the word *acyanopsia* highlights the importance of the first principle of this chapter: start with meaning. Why would you learn to spell a word if you don't know what it means? When would you ever use it? Not knowing what a word means actually makes it very difficult to spell. When you don't know the meaning of a word, you have no hooks upon which to hang the word's spelling.

Let's work through the spelling of *acyanopsia* by applying each of the teaching principles from this chapter.

Principle 1: Start with meaning

The word *acyanopsia* means 'unable to see the colour blue' or 'blue colour blindness'. Once you know *what* the word means, you are ready to understand how the word means. But understanding *how* the word makes its meaning isn't innate knowledge. We need someone to teach us – which brings us to Principle 2.

Principle 2: Teach spelling explicitly

This word requires some explicit teaching, as the meaningful parts of the word are not immediately obvious.

There are four morphemes, all borrowed from Greek:

1   a – a **prefix** meaning 'without'

2   cyan – a **free morpheme** meaning 'a shade of blue'. It is one of the three coloured inks in the printer cartridge, alongside magenta and yellow

3   ops – a **bound morpheme** meaning 'sight'.

4   ia – a noun forming suffix meaning 'the condition of'

Principle 3: Teach a repertoire of spelling knowledge

When you tried to spell *acyanopsia*, if you didn't know the meaning of the word you probably tried to write down the sounds you could hear. And that was probably hard because you don't know how the word is pronounced. In any case, sounds are an unreliable guide in English. You may have been correct with the first and last sounds of the word, but there were too many possible ways to write the sounds in the middle of the word. The odds of picking all the right letters for the sounds you can hear are slim. Perhaps you heard 'ak – yanop – sia' when you read the word. If someone had dictated the word to you, you would have heard 'ass – ion – opsia'

You need to draw upon a repertoire of spelling knowledge to spell a word correctly – one source is rarely enough. Knowing the word means 'not being able to see the colour blue' helps to identify the prefix 'a' at the beginning and the 'ops' at the end. You may remember seeing 'cyan' on a printer ink cartridge. Alternatively, if you've had a good spelling teacher in the lead-up to this spelling test, you may remember being taught that *cyan* is a Greek-origin word and has a letter pattern 'cy' making a sound like 'sigh', and is found in other Greek-origin words like *cycle* and *Cyclopes*.

We need to bring all our knowledge to the task of spelling, but we can use a range of strategies only if we have been taught a range of strategies.

Principle 4: Use an integrated approach to teaching spelling

You may not need to use *acyanopsia* very often in your writing, but learning to spell it has taught a lot that can be applied to other words. This helps you to spell words when you write and to understand new words when you read them.

Knowing that 'a' means 'without' helps us to understand the meaning of the word *amoral*: a – moral, without morals. It also helps to understand why that word is not spelled 'ammoral'.

Knowing that 'cyan' means blue may make us curious about the word *cyanide*, which is a poison that was first made by heating Prussian blue pigment powder, and tests for cyanide poisoning turn blue when positive.

The bound morpheme 'ops' and its relative 'opt' are very useful for understanding the meaning and spelling of many words, from *optician* (someone who works with sight) to *synoptic* (a general overview). It also helps us understand the origin and meaning of *autopsy*: 'auto – opsy', seeing with my own eyes.

The suffix 'ia' is used to describe many a medical condition from *dyslexia* to *hyperthermia*. The affix and base word tables in Appendix 2 will help you understand how the words dys-lex-ia and hyper-therm-ia make their meanings.

Chapter 4
Planning a spelling program

4

Learning objectives

After studying this chapter, you should be able to:

- develop a spelling program that teaches a repertoire of spelling knowledge

- plan activities that teach spelling across the curriculum

- answer the most common concerns people have about planning an effective spelling program.

Introduction

> I was wondering if you had any practical suggestions or ideas for addressing spelling in the classroom. You mention the importance of teaching the meaning of words and specifically fascinating and exciting students with the prospect of learning about new words. However, I am not quite sure how to implement this within the classroom.

THIS QUERY FROM a classroom teacher is a common one. Parents and teachers are very interested in pursuing a new approach to teaching spelling but can't quite see how it would look in practice. After all, it is one thing to theorise about what constitutes a good spelling program and another altogether to turn the theory into practice.

Chapter 3 outlined four key principles for teaching spelling: start with meaning; teach spelling explicitly; teach a repertoire of spelling knowledge; and integrate spelling instruction into all subject areas. This chapter introduces a 10-step process for planning and implementing a spelling program that is grounded in those four principles. Interspersed among the steps in the planning process are some of the questions teachers and parents frequently ask as they embark on the implementation process. What would your answers be? My responses are posted at the end of the chapter.

An overview of the 10-step planning process

1 **Remember the principles.** Teach a repertoire of spelling knowledge, and be meaning focused, explicit and integrated.

2 **Understand what is plausible for your year level.** Have high expectations – check what the curriculum documents recommend but don't be restricted by them.

3 **Examine words in context.** Investigate words in the places where they are doing their real work – communicating meaning in authentic writing, and not sitting alone and disconnected in spelling lists.

4 **Plan for explicit teaching but be prepared for incidental teaching.** Plan a program for teaching spelling knowledge, but be prepared to innovate on the plan as the students' needs and interests highlight gaps and opportunities.

5 **Select words that allow you to teach a range of skills.** Spelling programs should do more than teach spelling knowledge. They can build vocabulary and grammar knowledge, as well as teach conceptual knowledge within the disciplines.

6 **Explore the words through each spelling knowledge: etymology, morphology, orthography and phonology.** Apply these multiple lenses to the words you teach in your spelling program, giving the students multiple ways into understanding words and how they are spelled.

7 **Build students' meta-awareness of words.** Thinking about and discussing words, and their linguistic features, strengthens students' capacity to generalise newly learned spelling knowledge and instils a sense of responsibility for spelling words correctly.

8 **Practise spelling in authentic contexts**. Give the students multiple real and purposeful opportunities to see and use the words and the spelling strategies they have learned.

9 **Assess their spelling in use.** Look at students' writing to see what they can do in their spelling, as well as what they still need to learn.

10 **Keep records of your teaching and their learning.** Student progress must be recorded, alongside a record of which strategies and spelling knowledge have been taught.

This chapter focuses on Steps 1–8. Steps 9 and 10 are explored in detail in chapter 5, which covers assessment in spelling.

The steps in detail

1 Remember the principles

The aim is to develop a spelling program that explicitly builds a repertoire of spelling skills through the exploration of words encountered throughout the curriculum. Ensuring students know the meaning of the words is an absolute prerequisite for any spelling work. These principles provide touchstones for the development and implementation of your own spelling program.

- -

Question

It seems like a lot of work, and I'm not confident I have the linguistic knowledge, or the time, to write my own program. Why not just use an existing commercial spelling program?

What is your response to this question?

- -

2 Understand what is plausible for your year level

Curriculum documents rarely describe the development of a repertoire of spelling skills across all grades. They usually restrict young students to phonics work and sight words, and reserve morphological and etymological studies for the upper years of primary and secondary school. Too often they reflect an outdated developmental understanding of students' linguistic competence, rather than evidence-based understandings of what students can do with language, particularly when provided with explicit instruction. As Levesque, Breadmore and Deacon (2021) note, current popular models of reading and spelling instruction have not kept pace with the abundant recent research which describes the fundamental role morphological and orthographical knowledge play in the reading and writing process.

Appendix 4 contains a Scope and Sequence document describing a repertoire approach to spelling, from kindergarten through to the secondary years. It describes a base level of linguistic competence for each year level, but teachers should not be restricted by the descriptors. If students can do more than what is indicated in the document, then they should do more. Programming should follow the principles of a spiral curriculum. Strategies learned in one term should be revisited and applied again and again to other words throughout the school years.

COURAGEOUS TEACHING

Breadth of vocabulary is a better predictor of students' linguistic capabilities than age is. So teaching spelling through vocabulary, and teaching vocabulary through spelling, is more relevant to planning a spelling program than being restricted by what we think our age group is capable of.

Consider this example of Year 2 (seven-year-olds) participating in a school program on resilience. One of the key words in the program is *courageous*. Traditional spelling programs wouldn't consider teaching this word until perhaps Years 5 and 6. Even the Scope and Sequence in this book describes 'ous' as a more abstract Latin ending more easily introduced in Year 3. However, the word is being encountered repeatedly and in meaningful ways in the Year 2 curriculum in this school. It makes sense to look at how the word's meaning is made through its spelling.

The base word is *courage* – a noun. The suffix 'ous' turns the base noun into an adjective, giving us a word that can describe a person's characteristics. There is a further base word within *courage* – 'cour'. 'Cour' is a **morpheme**, but it is a French morpheme. It is from the French word *coeur*, which means heart, and this knowledge gives a deeper and more nuanced understanding of what *courageous* means, particularly in the context of a program seeking to build resilience.

This work on the suffix 'ous' in Year 2 doesn't mean that the Year 3 teachers' work is done for them. It means the Year 3 teachers have an excellent foundation upon which to consolidate the students' understanding of the 'ous' suffix, as they examine its use in other words that appear during the delivery of their Year 3 curriculum. 'Ous' is, after all, in the top twenty most commonly used suffixes (Cobb & Laufer 2021) so it is bound to make many appearances through the school years and across subject areas, from *famous* to *synonymous* and *numerous* words in between.

Question

What about the students who are performing below the suggested level in the Scope and Sequence for the grade level?

What would be your response to this question?

3 Examine words in context

The teaching of spelling should always be in the context of the words doing their job: communicating meaning.

Fortunately, words are working hard everywhere, so spelling can and should occur at any time in the school curriculum. You can examine words from a class novel, or from the science textbook chapter on electromagnetism. You can look at words in mathematics worksheets or in the video games that students play. The advantage of working with words in context is that the students will understand their meaning – the prerequisite principle of any spelling instruction.

4 Plan for explicit teaching but be prepared for incidental teaching

Spelling instruction should be planned for, but a repertoire approach to spelling gives rise to as much incidental teaching as it does planned teaching. The students become very tuned into words through the explicit planned teaching of spelling, and they begin to notice and question the spelling of words throughout the school day, which offers many opportunities for incidental teaching.

Planned explicit teaching

Most of the spelling teaching in your program will be done with the whole class. Even students who struggle with phonological knowledge, for example some dyslexic students, will benefit greatly, perhaps more so, from instruction in morphological and etymological knowledge. In traditional spelling programs they are often excluded from these interesting conversations about words because they are stuck in a phonological spelling stage they simply cannot graduate from.

Diagnostic assessment of students (see chapter 5 for details) may indicate that some students have gaps in their spelling knowledge, and these students can be placed in small groups to address those gaps. However, this small group focus work should be an adjunct to whole class work and not a replacement.

Table 4.1 describes the stages in an explicit spelling lesson teaching the prefix 'multi'. This is a model that can be used for both whole class and small group planned teaching.

5 Select words to build spelling, vocabulary, language and conceptual knowledge

Our spelling program aims to teach spelling strategies rather than spelling words, because with hundreds and thousands of words in the English language, learning each individual word is impossible. Nonetheless, we do need words to apply the spelling strategies to, so select words the students use a lot, as well as the words they need to succeed in school. The spelling program can do some heavy lifting throughout the curriculum. In addition to spelling knowledge, thoughtfully selected words can also build vocabulary, language and conceptual knowledge.

Table 4.2 is an example of a Year 1 teacher's selection of words for her spelling program. She has started by looking at what spelling knowledge is plausible for her year level (Step 2), and then sought words from

Table 4.1 Planning explicit teaching episodes

Stage	For example in Year 2
1 Identify spelling knowledge to be taught and apply to words being used in classroom teaching	**Year 2 Morphology** *Recognise and know how to use commonly used* **derivational prefixes** *with less transparent meanings* For example, apply this to the word multiply, which is being used frequently in the mathematics curriculum at this year level Teach the meaning of 'multi' = many
2 When applying the focus spelling knowledge to the selected word, consider other linguistic features of the word, to give the students a repertoire of ways into the spelling of the specific word	**Morphology** **Revision of Year 1 spelling knowledge** *Recognise and understand the morphemes in less obvious but commonly used compound words where the pronunciation of the base words remains the same* 'ply' is the other **morpheme** in multiply **Etymology** **Year 2 spelling knowledge** *Recognise and use words which come from other languages in words they use in other curriculum areas* 'ply' is from Latin, and it means 'fold'. We can see this meaning in words like plywood and three-ply wool **Phonology** **Revision of Year 1 spelling knowledge** *Recognise and use the* **consonant blends** *Recognise and use common long vowel patterns.* 'ply' contains a consonant blend 'pl', and 'y' is making the long 'i' **phoneme**
3 Whole-class demonstration of applying the focus linguistic knowledge to another word	Show students another example of how the prefix 'multi' applies to another common word, for example *multicoloured*. Write the prefix 'multi' in a different colour
4 Pair or individual work to apply the focus knowledge to other words. For younger students words will follow the linguistic pattern; for older students the words may prompt them to problem solve and make further hypotheses about the generalisability of the learned linguistic feature	Reinforce meaning by setting a task that demonstrates understanding of the new linguistic knowledge For example, students write their new base word e.g. 'millionaire', and illustrate it. They then add the prefix *multi* to make the base word read 'multimillionaire'. How does their illustration need to change to reflect the new word they have made?
5 Teacher-led discussion to tie up the lesson and summarise how the newly learned spelling knowledge works, and how it may be useful when attempting to spell other words	Record this lesson on a class word wall, or in a spelling journal (see Step 7 in the planning process). Revisit and reinforce this new spelling knowledge as it is encountered throughout the curriculum, for example '*multi*sided' objects in maths, and over the school year, for example, when celebrating '*multi*culturalism'

Source: Adapted from Apel, Masterson & Hart 2004: 301.

Table 4.2 Word selection for a spelling program

Morphology	Phonology	Orthography	Etymology	Visual
Compound words	*Onset and rime Digraphs Blends*	*Doubling Consonants*	*Words from other languages*	*Common sight words*
star fish	s – and	digging	magic	the
drift wood	sh – ell	trapped	beast	our
in side	s – un		tangerine	and
	sw – im		bask	we
	p – ool		castle	go
	l – id			of
	m – oat			to
Inflectional suffixes	*Long vowel silent e*	*Silent letters*		
horse –s	wave	castle		
shell – s	wide			
wash –ed	wine			
trap (p) –ed				

Source: Courtesy of Rose Patrick, a teacher in the Australian Capital Territory.

the picture book *Magic Beach* by Alison Lester, the book she was using as the focus for an inquiry unit on the sea (Step 3).

Spelling knowledge

Look for words that allow students to develop the full repertoire of spelling knowledge. Select words because of the affordances they offer in developing knowledge and skills that the students can apply to other words. The teacher selected *starfish* not because of a conviction that all six-year-olds should know how to spell *starfish*, but rather because it offers the opportunity to teach that English words can be made up of meaningful parts – morphemes. It also reinforces important phonological knowledge – the consonant blend 'st', the digraph 'sh' and the common rime patterns 'ar' and 'ish'.

Q. WHAT DO YOU CALL A SMALL WORD INSIDE ANOTHER WORD?

A. A coincidence

Bella is a Year 2 student who noticed that the word *crawl* contains the word *raw*, and she asked whether there is a special name for a word inside another word. This is the kind of thing that students start to notice about words once they have been alerted to new ways of thinking about words. It is a great example of being ready for incidental teaching. The teacher's response may have sounded something like this: 'Great question, Bella. As it turns out, there is no special name for this – except "coincidence"! That just means there is no reason for the word *raw* to be inside *crawl*. It is just random.'

However, sometimes there is a very good reason why there are words inside other words. For example, *breakfast* is made from the words *break* and *fast*, and that isn't random or a coincidence. These two words tell us what breakfast actually means: to break our fast when we wake up in the morning. (*Fast* can mean 'not eating'.)

These words inside a bigger word *do* have a special name: morpheme. That means that the smaller words you can see within the big word are important to the meaning of that big word. So you can see why 'raw' isn't a morpheme in 'crawl' – because 'raw' isn't important to the meaning of 'crawl'.

Here is another word with 'raw' in it: *rawhide*. I wonder whether our class can figure out whether 'raw' is a morpheme or a coincidence in this word. First, we will have to find out what *rawhide* means . . .

Vocabulary knowledge

Look for words that provide the foundation blocks for building students' vocabularies. The teacher's selection of words like *beast* and *bask* are opportunities to learn words that are not part of students' oral repertoires but are to be found in literary and academic texts. The compound word *inside* offers the opportunity to learn other compound words with the morpheme 'side', like *offside, outside* and *beside*.

Language knowledge

Look for words that teach the students about how the English language works, for example the *inflectional suffix 'ed'* marking the past tense in 'trapp*ed*' and 'wash*ed*'. Note how the 'ed' suffix is written the same in both words despite making different sounds 't' in trapped and 'd' in washed.

Conceptual knowledge

Look for words where the spelling helps teach the underlying concept of the word, for example the word *courageous* given earlier in the chapter, meaning 'full of heart', or the mathematical and scientific examples given in previous chapters, for example *perimeter* meaning 'measuring around'.

6 Explore the words through multiple lenses of phonological, morphological, orthographical, etymological and visual knowledge

Not all words can be explored through all lenses, but most words have at least two routes into them. The more ways into a word that a student can be shown, the more likely they are to build a robust memory of both the spelling strategy and the words it has been applied to.

Table 4.3 illustrates Rose's teaching of morphological knowledge through the word *starfish*, as well as her application of a phonological lens to the word. The spelling activities demonstrate spelling instruction that is both meaningful and engaging while also being explicit and direct.

Appendix 3 applies multiple lenses to commonly misspelled words in student writing, as well as frequently used words in English.

7 Build students' meta-awareness of words

An important component of the spelling program is the development of meta-awareness skills in the students so they can apply knowledge learned in explicit teaching episodes to their own spelling efforts. Spelling journals (see Figure 4.1) and word walls (see Figure 4.2) are two ways to achieve this. Both should provide the students with prompts to think about how to spell the word correctly. The following headings could be used:

- Does the word have a base word or affixes that would help me? (morphology)
- Does the word have a history that would help me? (etymology)

Table 4.3 Applying multiple lenses to a word

Starfish

Focus: Morphology – compound words

- Look at the starfish in Alison Lester's picture book

- What do they look like? Why do you think they might be called 'starfish'?

- How many different words can you hear when we say 'starfish'?

- Hold up two cards with pictures of a star and a fish to represent the two separate words

- Flip each card over to show the word for each and hold them up together, explain that even though we can hear two different words in *starfish*, it is written as one word

- Get students to record this in their wordbooks, picture and word

- Explain that in English there are lots of words that have two words in them, and give some other examples of compound words with star in them, for example *starlight, stargaze, stardust, superstar*. Make the compound words by writing and drawing a star on one side of the page, and writing and illustrating the second word on the other side of the page.

Other pathways into the word: Phonology – consonant blends

- Look at *star*. What sounds can you hear at the beginning? 'St' How many sounds are there in 'st'? 's' and 't'

- Have two cards, one with 's' and the other 't', and say each sound individually. Then push the cards together, and ask the students to join the sounds together as the cards are pushed together.

- Take the 't' away. What sound is left? 's' Put the 't' back. What sounds can we hear now? 'st'

- What other words can we think of that have 'st' at the beginning? Record the words on a whiteboard, and write the 'st' in a different colour from the remainder of the word.

- Have students record two 'st' words of their choice in their word books and illustrate them.

Note: Part of the morphology example appeared in Adoniou 2014: 144–54.

- Are there other possible letter patterns for the sounds I can hear? (phonology)

- Is there a spelling rule that can help me? (orthography)

- Have I seen the word before? Where? (visual)

Students will use word walls and journals only if their teachers use them also, and their use must be a classroom expectation. Teachers should also model meta-awareness of words by thinking out loud about words using the same prompts.

Word	Does the word have a base word or affixes that would help me?	Are there other possible letter patterns for the sounds I can hear?	Is there a spelling rule that can help me?	Does the word have a history that would help me?	Have I seen the word before? Where?
beautiful	beauty + full	'eau' is making a 'you' sound	Change 'y' to 'i' when adding a suffix. When 'full' is added as a suffix it usually drops one 'l'	It's from the French. The modern French word for beautiful is 'beau'. That's why we have the letter pattern 'eau'	It's in lots of songs! Like One Direction's 'What makes you beautiful'

Figure 4.1 Student spelling journal

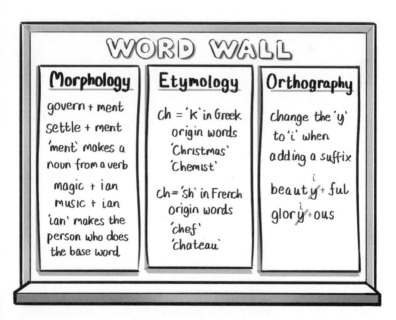

Figure 4.2 Classroom word wall

8 Practise spelling in authentic contexts

Give the students opportunities to use words for real purposes and to see words in multiple contexts. The students need plenty of opportunities for practice after learning a new word or strategy if they are to generalise learning successfully from planned explicit teaching to their own writing throughout other parts of the school day. One explicit teaching episode is unlikely to be sufficient, and it is important to incorporate contextual repetition into the spelling work.

- -

Question

We have been teaching the students about how words work, and they really love learning about words. But we do not see much transfer to their writing. What can we do?

What would your response to this question be?

- -

A SPELLING DETECTIVE GAME

Have one student think of a word that contains language features learned during the week, or draw one out of a hat. The student then becomes the word, and the class has to figure out their identity. No guessing – this is a game of deduction, and these are the questions to ask.

Can you deduce this word's identity?

Etymology
Q. Where are you from originally?
A. Greece
Q. What evidence do you have to prove it?
A. I have the letter pattern 'psy' in me

Morphology
Q. Are you alone or with colleagues/morphemes?
A. I have two morphemes, but they are not very common

Orthography
Q. Do you follow the rules?
A. I am not breaking any rules ...

Visual
Q. Do you have any distinguishing features?
A. I am quite a long word.

Semantics
Q. What is your purpose? What do you mean?
A. I am a doctor for your soul.

Responses to common questions from teachers and parents

- -

Question

It seems like a lot of work, and I'm not confident that I have the linguistic knowledge to write my own program. Why not just use an existing commercial spelling program?

- -

For those interested in a meaning-based repertoire approach to teaching spelling, there are no commercial spelling programs. There are many spelling programs that focus primarily on the development of phonological and orthographical spelling knowledge, for example Jolly Phonics, Sounds Write, Soundwaves. There are a smaller number of programs that describe a full range of spelling knowledge, for example Words Their Way. However, these programs teach spelling in a developmental manner; that is, the students must graduate through the spelling knowledge, starting with phonological and ending with etymological.

Additionally, commercial spelling programs are necessarily standardised, and inevitably present lists of words for students to work on. When spelling is delivered as a separate curriculum entity in this way, we lose the opportunity for deeper vocabulary and conceptual learning that occurs when we integrate our spelling program across the curriculum.

Decontextualised work on words is not helpful for many students, and does not respond to the diversity of students and curriculum contexts that educators work with. It is why traditional spelling programs are ineffective for so many students, and unsatisfying for so many teachers.

You do need to know a lot about words in order to develop your own spelling program, but in reality you need to know a lot about words in order to teach commercial spelling programs effectively as well. If we are going to improve our students' spelling outcomes, we must acknowledge that educators need to know more about how words work. Improved content knowledge of the linguistics of spelling, combined with teachers' own considerable knowledge of how best to engage their students in learning, is the best way to develop a spelling program that meets the needs of different learners in different teaching contexts.

- -

Question

What about the students who are performing below the suggested level in the Scope and Sequence for the grade level?

- -

Students who are underperforming in spelling are usually over relying on their phonological strategies; that is, when in doubt they sound out, and this inevitably leads them to the wrong spelling. Paradoxically, these students are then often placed in remedial phonics programs where they are given more intense phonological instruction. This is a very blunt assessment of their spelling abilities, and their placement in such programs means they miss out on instruction in the other areas of spelling knowledge.

The repertoire Scope and Sequence for spelling allows teachers to describe a more nuanced profile of their underachieving spellers, and to tailor instruction that does not require sending a student back to kindergarten-type phonics programs for spelling. A student may require some specialist support in one kind of spelling knowledge, but they can, and should, participate alongside their peers for the majority of the class spelling program.

Consider this example of a 13-year-old's spelling. Asked why she would like a horse as a pet, she wrote,

I would like a houese because they are cute and rilly helpfll and butterfoll.
[I would like a horse because they are cute and really helpful and beautiful.]

Her high school teacher is understandably concerned at this level of spelling. How will the student cope with the high school curriculum, let alone the standardised tests she will be subjected to? The teacher feels like she has to 'go back to the beginning' with the student and that she 'doesn't even know her sounds'. She wonders how she can possibly provide the support required given the time constraints of a high school curriculum and the limited opportunities for one-on-one support.

However, as poor as the student's spelling is, there isn't a need to start over. Her problem is not really her 'sounds'; in fact she has some sophisticated phonological and orthographical knowledge like 'ould', 'ause' and 'ute'. But she over-relies on sounds when in doubt, and most particularly when faced with multisyllable words. Apart from her spelling of 'horse', all of her other spelling errors are best dealt with through morphological instruction.

When spelling, she isn't thinking about what the word means, and how it makes its meaning, so when faced with a long word, she simply writes the sounds she can hear. So real + ly becomes r-i-l-l-y; a spelling that is not only phonologically possible but also follows an orthographical convention of doubling a consonant after a short vowel. However, it is not a spelling that reflects the meaning of the word – the adjective 'real' followed by the suffix 'ly' to turn it into an adverb.

Similarly, 'helpfll' and 'butterfoll' are spellings that reflect the student's pronunciation rather than her understanding of the words' meanings and how the spelling makes those meanings.

So, as poor as the student's spelling appears to be, she will not benefit from being placed in a back-to-basics phonics program. She would benefit from extra support in phonological and orthographical knowledge at about the Year 3 level described in the Scope and Sequence in Appendix 4, specifically, 'recognise and use less common graphemes with etymological explanations e.g. magic, beauty'. However, she should also participate in the whole class morphological and etymological instruction recommended for her grade in the Scope and Sequence.

- -

Question

We have been teaching the students about how words work, and they really love learning about words. But we do not see much transfer to their writing. What can we do?

- -

Students don't automatically see the link between spelling and writing, so it is necessary to rethink the way we talk about spelling. One suggestion is to not give it a delineated named place on the timetable. Having a time for spelling on the timetable encourages students to think of it as a subject, rather than a cross-curriculum skill. Be sure to 'do' spelling whenever and wherever you have words to investigate (i.e. any and all the time). Always emphasise that the point of spelling is to write so that others can comprehend, and not to achieve a mark on a spelling test.

It is hard to think through all of your spelling strategies while in the midst of the other demands that writing makes on your brain, for example ideas and grammar. So don't expect perfect spelling on the first draft, but do expect perfect spelling on the final draft. Have a spelling edit routine at the end of writing and make sure the students do that edit. Too often, final edits drop off the teacher's priority list, and instead teachers swoop in and do the corrections themselves. Make students use the spelling journals and word walls that have been set up, and make them take responsibility for getting their spelling right.

Finally, it takes time to develop new habits. If students haven't thought about words in this way before (and indeed most teachers haven't), it will take time for them to start using new strategies. Be patient and persistent, and put in place constant reminders of what their spelling strategies are: make them public on word walls, and use them yourself as you too solve your spelling dilemmas out loud for them.

Summary

I want my child to love language and to understand the meaning behind the words. Not just how to spell them from memory but to become an expert in language and how to use it.

This parent's vision for learning spelling is surely what we all want for the students we work with. An innovative and engaging approach to spelling can induce a love of the language and a life-long engagement with the written word, but as Apel, Masterson and Hart (2004) have noted, too often spelling programs are guided by tradition rather than innovation.

This chapter has described the ways in which teachers can combine linguistic knowledge of words with their well-established understandings of how students learn, to develop an innovative, repertoire-based spelling program that will engage students of all grades.

Chapter 5 looks at ways of ensuring that the spelling program does what it seeks to achieve: develop spelling experts who love language.

Chapter 5
Assessing spelling

5

Learning objectives

After studying this chapter, you should be able to:

- select words for spelling assessment
- diagnose spelling errors
- monitor student growth and understanding across spelling knowledge.

Introduction

> We are required to have spelling tests each week, which I think is outrageous because we don't actually teach spelling during the week. We hand out words on Monday and test them on Friday – it is just a ritual.
>
> A TEACHER

> My daughter does OK in the spelling tests each week – after much painful rote learning. But they have no impact on her spelling outside that context.
>
> A PARENT

THESE COMMENTS WILL be familiar to many teachers and parents. The spelling test is a staple of classroom practice, but it is difficult to see its purpose if it is not improving spelling skills. For those who struggle with spelling, the test merely serves as a weekly reminder of their inadequacies. This is not to say we shouldn't assess spelling – the assessment of spelling is crucial to the improvement of spelling. However, the traditional weekly spelling test is not an instructive assessment; it has simply become a routine embedded into the teaching psyche of many.

Assessing spelling

This chapter is focused on getting spelling assessment right, and expands upon Steps 9 and 10 in the program planning process, introduced in chapter 4: assessing spelling in use, and keeping records of teaching and learning.

9 Assessing spelling in use

Traditionally, spelling has been assessed through a list of words given at the end of the week, or sometimes a dictation passage with target words in it. Words are then marked as spelled correctly or incorrectly.

There are two key problems with this approach. First, such tests are a blunt instrument for assessing the complex set of linguistic skills that spelling is. Simply marking words as right or wrong fails to attend to that complexity. Second, whether a student can spell in a test is a moot point; the point of spelling is to communicate clearly with others. As many teachers and parents have observed, students can learn words for spelling tests, which they go on to spell incorrectly in the course of their everyday writing. Scoring well in a spelling test is ultimately of no use if the knowledge is not transferred beyond the test.

A more useful assessment approach will seek to understand:

1 whether students can spell in authentic communicative tasks, and

2 which spelling knowledge they use successfully, and which they struggle with.

Which words to assess?

Students' writing samples provide a legitimate source of spellings to assess. Importantly, these words show what resources students bring to the spelling task when they have to simultaneously attend to other aspects of the writing process, like composition, sentence structure and ideas (Apel, Masterson & Niessen 2004).

There is the risk that students will mask their spelling challenges in their writing by not attempting words they find difficult (Kohnen, Nickels & Castles 2009). To counter the possibility that poor spellers, in particular, might not attempt the variety of words required to give a full picture of their spelling needs, spelling inventories can supplement the words from student writing samples. Lists of words considered typical or desirable for a grade level are a helpful source when choosing words for an inventory. See for example the lists of 'basic', 'simple', 'difficult' and 'challenging' words in the 'Persuasive Writing Marking Guide' at www .nap.edu.au or the word lists in 'National curriculum in England: English programmes of study' at https://www.gov.uk/government/publications/ national-curriculum-in-england-english-programmes-of-study.

What are we assessing?

The purpose of assessing spelling is not to record how many words on a list students can spell. The purpose is to monitor student progress (and, by default, monitor our teaching methods) and to diagnose the spelling challenges of those students who are not progressing. However, while spelling is probably the most tested subject in schools, it is also the least diagnosed. Very little is done with the spelling data that is captured each Friday morning in classrooms around the globe. One study found that 42 per cent of teachers make no changes to their teaching practice as a result of spelling test results (Graham et al. 2008). Other research (Johnston 2001) found that when teachers were asked whether they changed their instructional practice as a result of spelling test results, 95 per cent said they did. However, when asked to explain how they changed their practice, they recounted ways in which they had adapted the test for the following week, for example, fewer words for less able students, or bonus words for better spellers. So the test did not inform teaching practice, it informed test construction.

Diagnosing spelling challenges

This book has described spelling as a complex linguistic skill – a tapestry of different spelling knowledge. Therefore an effective assessment of spelling must unpack the threads to establish where each student's capabilities are (Kohnen, Nickels & Castles 2009) and then build skills in their weak areas and capitalise on their strengths.

Students are capable of using all types of spelling knowledge at all stages of their spelling growth. Indeed, a characteristic of good spellers is their capacity to draw upon the full repertoire of spelling knowledge, so diagnostic analyses of spelling must take account of how students are using all linguistic resources in their spelling attempts.

The aim is not to look for evidence of a stage of spelling development and then to place the student in that stage, as is common in many spelling programs. If we focus on looking for specific stage-based behaviour, we can miss valuable information about the other kinds of language knowledge a student may or may not be using (Apel, Masterson & Niessen 2004). Instead, we need to look for evidence of spelling behaviour across the full repertoire of spelling knowledge. This allows teachers to understand *how* the students are making their errors rather than simply knowing that students are making errors. Understanding *how* allows us to hypothesise about *why* students make their errors, and then change our instruction accordingly.

The stages for diagnostic spelling assessment are:

1 understand *how* the errors are made

2 analyse the patterns that emerge from understanding *how* in order to establish *why*, and hypothesise about *why* each student makes errors of that kind

3 implement spelling instruction that tests the hypothesis

4 monitor spelling to see whether the new instruction is working (Apel, Masterson & Niessen 2004: 656).

Table 5.1 is a spelling diagnosis framework within which to record the first two stages of diagnostic spelling assessment: understanding *how* errors are made, and analysing *why*. The columns provide space for the analysis of the ways in which phonological, orthographical and morphological knowledge is evident in the students' spelling attempts. The etymology column is for the teacher's own notes on whether the etymology of the word would provide helpful information about its spelling that might address any gaps noted in the other three columns. The bottom row provides space for

Table 5.1 Spelling diagnosis framework

Actual word	Student spelling	Phonology	Morphology	Orthography	Etymology
		Is the spelling phonetically plausible?	Number of morphemes spelled correctly	Does the spelling demonstrate knowledge about letter pattern conventions?	Is there etymological knowledge that would help spell this word?
Total Number of instances out of possible number of instances					

tallying the instances of use for each spelling knowledge. These tallies help map patterns in each student's use of spelling knowledge.

A diagnosis of around 20 spelling errors, collected from writing and a spelling inventory, is sufficient to provide good insights into the spelling behaviour of students and to highlight where they require additional instruction.

'HORSES ARE BUTTERFOLL'

We saw 13-year-old Emily's writing in chapter 4. Her spelling of 'beautiful' is wrong, but what can the teacher do about it – besides correct the error? Emily has probably had such errors corrected for her through all her years of schooling, and it hasn't helped her spelling. She needs to be taught, and in order to teach her we need to understand how she made this error. What knowledge has she used? And which spelling knowledge has she not used?

Emily has relied on her **phonological** knowledge of how words work. She has used plausible letters for each of the sounds she can hear, including some less frequent graphemes for sounds, for example the 'u' for the 'you' sound she can hear at the beginning of the word beaut, as in 'cute'. She has even used some **orthographic** conventions, for example, the doubling of the 'l' after a short consonant sound in 'foll'.

She knows the meaning of the word, because she wants to tell us that, in her opinion, horses are beautiful. However, she did not use her knowledge of the meaning of the word to help her spell the word. She hasn't thought: 'What does this word mean?'; she has thought: 'What sounds can I hear?' She doesn't know the word is made of two **morphemes**: 'beauty' and 'ful', to mean 'full of beauty'. She doesn't know the **orthographical** convention of changing the 'y' to an 'i' on the end of the base morpheme before adding a suffix. She doesn't know the **orthographical** convention of dropping the 'l' on 'full' when using it as a suffix. She doesn't know that words have an **etymology** and that words can be borrowed from other languages and can bring their phonemic and graphemic patterns from those languages; for example 'eau' is a French representation of the sound she can hear in the first syllable of the word.

This diagnosis of how Emily has made her error provides very clear direction for what kind of explicit teaching she requires.

- -
Question
Table 5.2 contains a diagnosis of Emily's spelling of the word *beautiful* using the spelling diagnosis framework. Can you complete the table for her other errors taken from the same piece of writing? On this sample of errors, what can you say about why she is making these errors, and what spelling instruction do you suggest? Compare your thoughts with the suggestions made at the end of the chapter.
- -

What we learn from diagnostic assessment
Diagnostic assessment allows us to see the ways students, both struggling and proficient spellers, approach spelling. It provides valuable information about which linguistic resources a student is using and which they are not. The close observation of *how* the errors are being made allows us to consider *why* they are being made.

Table 5.2 Spelling diagnosis framework – Emily

Actual word	Student spelling	Phonology	Morphology	Orthography	Etymology teacher note
		Is the spelling phonetically plausible?	Number of morphemes spelled correctly	Does the spelling demonstrate knowledge about letter pattern conventions?	Is there etymological knowledge that would help spell this word?
beautiful	butterfoll	yes	0/2 base = beauty suffix = ful	Partial	eau = French letter pattern
helpful really scared	helpfll rilly sced				
Total Number of instances out of possible number of instances					

Often, struggling spellers have only one resource to draw upon: the phonological. Analysis of their spelling indicates that they are successful when letters match the sounds in a consistent manner. However, success with this phonological skill is also responsible for all of their spelling errors. In other words, sounding out is their predominant strategy, and given the poor phonetic match between sounds and symbols in English, it results in more misspellings than correct spellings.

Conversely, analyses can also show when a student has weak phonological knowledge, using implausible or incorrect letters, which can indicate an overreliance on their visual memory, or a challenge with phonemic awareness; that is, they are struggling to hear the sounds in words, and may benefit from activities designed to improve phonemic awareness.

With a more nuanced diagnosis of the spelling knowledge a student uses, teachers can devise instruction that both targets the weak areas and plays to the strengths the students display in their approach to words.

The aim of the assessment is to inform spelling instruction that builds a robust repertoire of spelling knowledge in all students.

A formal diagnosis of spelling errors conducted at the beginning of the year provides enough information to inform the content of a six-month program of spelling instruction. Mid-way through the school year, a comprehensive diagnostic analysis can be repeated to chart growth, and make any necessary adjustments to instruction for the following six months.

Monitoring spelling

In between the diagnostic assessments, spelling skills need to be taught and students' spelling must be monitored and their progress recorded. This formative assessment, along with good record-keeping, is key to developing a spelling program that is responsive to students' needs and abilities.

10 Keep records of your teaching and their learning

The Spelling Scope and Sequence (see Appendix 4), student interests and the diagnosis of their spelling behaviour all guide the content of the spelling program, as described in chapter 4. Records then need to be kept to show how each student is achieving against the teaching of that content. We need to be able to answer the questions:

1   Are students learning how words work?

2   Are they applying this knowledge to other words?

Table 5.3 presents a format for recording the teaching and learning that happens through the year and how each student is achieving. A cross (X) could indicate full achievement while a forward slash (/) could indicate partial achievement. For example, the student may have written the suffix as both 'ful' and 'full' in their written work. Robust understandings of new spelling knowledge are evidenced in multiple ways, so the columns provide the space for recording student learning as it is observed in

Table 5.3 Recording teaching and learning – example: meaning and use of suffix 'ful'

Spelling knowledge	Student's name	Evidenced in explicit teaching	Evidenced in authentic writing	Evidenced in talk[1]	Evidenced in formal assessments[2]
The suffix 'ful'	Emily	X	/	X	X

[1] That is, meta-awareness.
[2] For example, diagnostic or standardised tests.

different contexts. For example, do they show understanding of the taught knowledge during the explicit teaching activities? Is there evidence of them applying that knowledge when they are engaged in everyday writing? Do they talk about words in different ways? Do they notice features in words? And do formal assessments show improved spelling and an increased use of a repertoire of spelling knowledge?

SPELLING: EVERYONE'S RESPONSIBILITY

All teachers should be involved in the teaching and monitoring of spelling, and schools should agree on a uniform approach to talking about words in all disciplines.

Every teacher should introduce new content vocabulary in a way that highlights the linguistic threads within the word, supporting both the comprehension and the correct spelling of the word. And schools should use a whole school approach to the instructive correction of spelling errors, using a consistent editing system that supports students to take responsibility for correcting their own errors, no matter which class they are attending or which teacher they have. For example, with the 'POEM' proofing code, teachers underline the incorrectly spelled component of the word and provide a coded prompt for getting the word right.

- /P phonology = this phoneme is represented by a different grapheme
- /O orthography = this morpheme or phoneme follows a spelling convention

- /E etymology = this morpheme, syllable or phoneme has a Greek/Latin/French etc. origin
- /M morphology = this word is made from morphemes

For example, if the student has written brekfast, the teacher puts a slash to indicate the two morphemes: brek/fast, and marks an M above the incorrectly spelled morpheme.

If the student has written 'fisical' for 'physical', the teacher puts a slash behind the opening syllable: fi/sical, and marks it with an E, and a clue (Greek) to prompt the student to find the correct spelling: phy/sical.

The students can then record this learning in their spelling journals or on a word wall, as described in Step 7 of the planning process outlined in chapter 4.

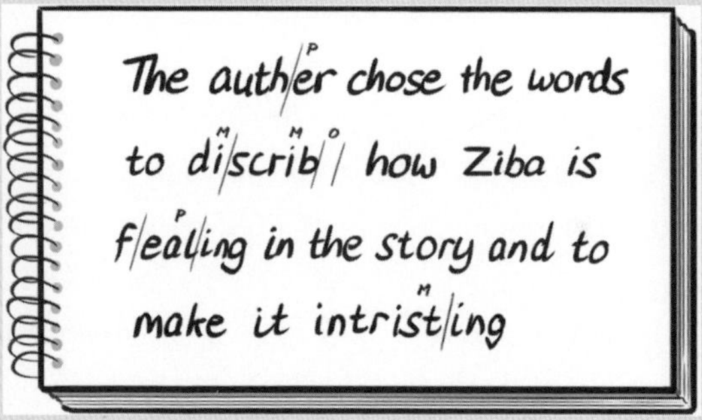

The auth/er chose the words to di/scrib/ how Ziba is f/eal/ing in the story and to make it intrist/ing

Figure 5.1   Example of the spelling proofreading code

Conclusion

We need to be teachers, not copy-editors

Many of us correct spelling, even those not involved with teaching children. We snigger at the misspelled items on the restaurant menu or in the real estate advertisements. We tut-tut at the spelling errors in the newspaper, or on the captions that accompany our TV news. Meanwhile we remain blissfully blind to our own fossilised spelling errors.

The capacity to spot and correct spelling errors is insufficient for anyone interested in teaching students to spell, because correcting spelling is not teaching spelling – it is copy-editing. Yet this is how we have traditionally approached assessment in spelling. So we are left with the rather sad reality that although very few teachers actually teach spelling, almost all test it, and then do very little with the information embedded in those test results. Spelling is simply considered a convention to mark as correct or incorrect (Apel, Masterson & Hart 2004) rather than a linguistic skill that provides insights into the linguistic development of the student (Apel, Masterson & Niessen 2004, Arndt & Foorman 2010, Boynton Hauerwas & Walker 2004).

Spelling: The last frontier?

This final chapter has provided an alternative vision and framework for the assessment of spelling skills, and brings the book to its logical conclusion. I began the book by suggesting that poor spelling is a consequence of uninformed teaching. Spelling appears to be the last frontier of literacy teaching. While there are many examples of literacy programs that teach reading and writing in meaningful and engaging ways, spelling seems to have been left off the reform agenda. Instead, rote learning and spelling tests have been the mainstay of spelling instruction because English spelling has been characterised as inexplicable and unteachable. In this book I have sought to set that record straight: English spelling is explicable, and not only is it teachable but it is also a pleasure to teach and a joy to learn. It is time we conquered this last frontier, and it is my hope that this book will be a trusty companion on that journey.

Case study questions

1 How did you analyse Emily's errors?
2 What did her errors tell you about her spelling knowledge?
3 What type of instruction would she benefit from?

Answers

1 How Emily is making her errors?

Actual word	Student spelling	Phonology	Morphology	Orthography	Etymology teacher note
		Is the spelling phonetically plausible?	Number of morphemes spelled correctly	Does the spelling demonstrate knowledge about letter patterns?	Is there etymological knowledge that would help spell this word?
beautiful	butterfoll	yes	0/2 Base – beauty Suffix – ful	partial	eau – French pattern
helpful	helpfll	yes	1/2 Base – help Suffix – ful	yes	N/A
really	rilly	yes	0/2 Base – real Suffix – ly	yes NB: the student's use of -ly on the end is not a recognition of a suffix but an application of an orthographic understanding of doubling the consonant after a short vowel, e.g. silly	The vowel digraph 'ea' was originally pronounced as two separate vowel sounds, as can be heard in the related word 'reality'
scared	sced	yes	0/2 Base – scare Suffix – ed	partial – use of blend 'sc' NB: the student's use of -ed on the end is not a recognition of a suffix but an application of her phonological knowledge	N/A
Total Number of instances out of possible number of instances		**4/4**	**1/8**	**2.5/4**	

2 **Why** is Emily making the errors? The analysis of these indicative spelling errors shows Emily has one reasonably well-developed spelling strategy: phonological knowledge. She has some basic orthographical knowledge and no morphological knowledge or etymological insights.

3 **What** is the teaching solution? Not a phonics program, which is what her school was considering. As research has found, spelling instruction that focuses solely on the phonological will lead to improvements in phonological awareness, but not in spelling development (Apel, Masterson & Hart 2004). Emily's error patterns show that she needs instruction in all other spelling knowledge if she is going to improve in her spelling.

- -

Appendix 1

Some stories about words

Almost every word tells a story. Here are just a few to get you started with your own investigations.

Why is that letter there?

The printing press

Before 1500, English texts were handwritten by monks and scribes who spelled words the way they pronounced them, so spelling varied from book to book, and even person to person. But the arrival of the first printing press in England helped to change that.

William Caxton, an Englishman, imported the printing press from Europe, and he also imported Flemish labourers to work the presses, as nobody in England had the skills. The Flemish workers didn't speak English, and they were also a little creative with their typesetting. In order to justify the print on the page so that it looked orderly and neat, they added letters here and there – a double consonant here, an 'e' on the end of a word there. They also opted to spell some English words in a Flemish way, including putting in an 'h' after the 'g' in *ghost*, *ghastly* and *aghast* – words that had been *gost*, *gastly* and *agast* until then.

Cultural cringe?

Also during this time of spelling standardisation it was decided that some words which had long-forgotten Latin roots should be reintroduced to those roots. So *debt* had come from the Latin 'debitum', from which we more obviously have the word 'debit' as in debit card. But it had for many hundreds of years been pronounced without the 'b' and spelled 'dette'. The 'b' was restored to remind us of the origin of the word. This also explains the 'p' in *receipt*, the 'c' in *scissors* and some other 'silent' letters.

We could regard this as a bit of sixteenth-century snobbery that has contrived to make spelling difficult for twenty-first-century learners, but really they were just trying to put meaning clues back into spelling.

It just looks neater . . .

Should is the past of *shall*, and *would* is the past of *will*. It is possible to see where the 'l' in *should* and *would* has come from; imagine them as *shalled* and *willed*, and you can hear how those silent 'l's were once pronounced. But that doesn't explain the silent 'l' in *could*, which is the past of *can*. The spelling of *could* simply fell into line with *should* or *would* – it just looked neater!

Foreign is another example of a word that has fallen into line with other spellings. In 1300 it was spelled variously as *foran, forain* and *foreyne*. In 1700 the spelling became standardised as 'foreign', copying a French spelling pattern that was considered to be more cultural, and mimicked other French import words like *reign* and *sovereign*.

We used to say it

As we saw with *should* and *would*, very often the silent letters in words are ones we used to pronounce – in words like *light* and *night*, or *comb* and *climb*. The 'gh' was pronounced much like the 'ch' on the end of *loch*, and there are still some dialects of English where the guttural 'gh' can still be heard. You can still hear the 'b' in *climb* in the word *clamber*, just as you can still hear the 'g' in *sign* in *signal* and *signature*.

Right up until the twentieth century many thought you were uncouth if you didn't pronounce the 'l' in *would*, in much the same way that there is still a prejudice against those who drop their 'h's in 'hospital', for example.

Words brought back from travels

By the 1700s English explorers were travelling the globe and bringing back new objects previously unknown in England. In the absence of an existing English word they adopted their indigenous names, and new letter patterns were introduced to English spelling as a result. Many thousands of words came into English this way, from *kangaroo* and *koala* to *kayak* and *khaki* (the Urdu word for dusty).

Kayak is an Inuit word meaning small boat made from skins, and *dinghy* is the Hindi word for a small boat. *Catamaran* is from the Tamil compound word *kattu-maram*, meaning tied wood, and see chapter 1 for the story of *yacht*. *Shampoo* was a Hindi word for a type of massage, and the drink we know as *punch* was a Sanskrit word for a combination of five nectars of the gods. Many new food names arrived as well, from Italian *spaghetti* (little strings) to *mocha*, named for the Yemeni port Mocha from where coffee was exported.

Named after ...

Macadamia nuts were named after a Scottish-born scientist living in Australia, John Macadam. Another John McAdam gave his name to *tarmac*, originally called tar macadam. Macadam was the process he had invented for laying gravel on roads.

Franz Anton Mesmer was famous in the 1700s for his hypnotic treatment of patients with a technique that became known as *mesmerising*. *Sideburns* are named after the American general Ambrose Everett Burnside, who was famous for his distinctive facial hair, which he grew from in front of his ears to join his moustache. They were originally known as burnsides, but later reversed to become sideburns.

The loose pants we know as *bloomers* were named after Amelia Jenks Bloomer, an American suffragette who championed women's rights. One of her causes was to lobby for clothing for women that didn't restrict their activities. Although she didn't invent bloomers or even wear them, they were named for her.

Jules Leotard was a French trapeze artist who wore a skin-tight costume, now known as a *leotard*. The *cardigan* was named for a British general, the Earl of Cardigan, who apparently liked the style of the woollen, buttoned jumper so much that he wore it into battle. *Denim* describes the fabric used for making jeans – a fabric that came from a town called Nimes in France; hence it was de Nime. The *bikini* was named by a French fashion designer. The two-piece swimming costume was already in existence, but it was thought that the garment would receive publicity if named for the South Pacific Bikini atoll where the United States had just detonated an atomic bomb. And they were right.

Sounds like ...

Many English words are onomatopoeic – words that sound like what they are naming, like *zip* and *whiz*. Perhaps it isn't surprising that many of the words that describe the noises we make are onomatopoeic, for example *giggle, titter, guffaw, shriek, screech, roar, sniff* and *chatter*. Sometimes the onomatopoeic roots of words have become obscured. *Laugh* has an onomatopoeic root: *lach*, pronounced with the guttural 'ch' on the end of *loch*, as was the 'gh' on the end of *cough*.

Colourful words

White is an Old English word originally written and pronounced 'hwit' – see the story about what, where, why and when in chapter 2. But we have imported lots of other white words into English from other languages.

The white whale we call *beluga* is from Russian, with the Russian morpheme 'bel' meaning 'white'. We can also see it in Belarus, which means 'white Russia'.

Blancmange is a sweet milky jelly, and a compound word from the French: *blanc* and *mange*, meaning 'white eating'. It used to be made from an exotic collection of white ingredients that included white chicken meat, rice, cream, almonds and sugar.

Albinos are those who have a lack of melanin in their skins, which makes them very pale. The word comes from the Latin *albus*, which means 'white'. This is the same root that gives us *album*, originally a blank or white tablet for writing. It even gives us the name of the city Albuquerque in the United States, a combination of *albus* and *quercus* – oak.

The Chinese cabbage *bok choy* is 'white vegetable' in Chinese. And the illness *leukaemia*, which causes a large number of white blood cells to develop, is a compound of two Greek words: *leuko* – white, and *aemia* – blood.

Mythical words

Titans were a mythological race of giants in Ancient Greece. They have found their way into everyday language via the name of the most famous ship of all, the *Titanic*, as well as the chemical element *titanium*, named for its extreme strength. The most famous of all the ancient Greek Titans was Atlas. His task was to carry the sky on his shoulders, and he gives his name to the *atlas*, the book that carries the whole world within it.

Pan was a half man, half goat shepherd god. He gave his name to *pan pipes*, which apparently were his instrument of choice. He also liked to scare and trick people as he roamed his fields, causing *panic*.

Echo was a beautiful Greek nymph who was cursed by a powerful Greek goddess. The curse meant that Echo lost her own voice and could only repeat the words of others, so it is easy to see where we get our word for *echo* from! Echo fell in love with a young man named *Narcissus*. But Narcissus was in love with himself – hence our modern word *narcissistic* for people obsessed with themselves. Narcissus eventually died because he couldn't tear himself away from his own reflection in a pond. Where he died, daffodils grew – and the botanical name for the daffodil is *Narcissus*.

The *echidna* is an egg-laying mammal – a confusing mix for the scientists who first described it. They named it after the equally unusual Echidna from Greek mythology. She was a nymph who has half woman, half snake.

Flora and fauna

What do *garlic, garfish* and *Edgar* have in common? The morpheme 'gar', meaning spear. So garlic is a spear-shaped leek, garfish are spear-shaped fish and Ed meant prosperity – so Edgar is a wealthy warrior.

Tulips may be famous in Holland, but they are native to Turkey, which is where the name comes from. *Tülbent* is the Turkish word for 'turban', and that is what the flowers were thought to look like.

Chrysanthemum may be a long word, but in the end it is just a golden flower. It is a compound of two Greek words: 'chrys' meaning gold, and 'anthemum' meaning flower. We can see 'anth' again in *anthology*, a collection of poems, or perhaps more poetically, a compound of 'anth' and 'ology' – words about flowers, or perhaps flowery words . . .

Mandarin was the name the Portuguese used to describe Chinese officials. It came from the Portuguese word *mandar*, meaning to command (which helps explain the origin of *command* too!). These Chinese officials wore deep orange robes, and so when the English were looking for a name for a small, deep orange fruit, they chose *mandarin*.

Spelling by numbers

A *siesta* is a midday nap, and the word has come from Latin via Spanish. Its origin is in the Latin for the sixth hour after sunrise – midday, and the Spanish word for six is *seis*.

Google is a made-up name, inspired by another made-up word: *googol*, the word for a number represented by the numeral 1 followed by 100 zeros. Googol was coined by an American mathematician who asked his young nephew to make up a name for a really big number.

Two has that silent w, but you can hear it in other related words: *twin, twice, between*. Another word for two is *duo*, and that is from the Latin word *due*. We can see this word in *duet*, but it is even hiding in the word *dubious* – which means to hesitate between two opinions. And it is there in *double, duplicate* and *duplex*.

Portmanteaus

Splurge has an onomatopoeic ring to it as well as a blend of *splash* and *surge*. *Velcro* is a blend of two French words: *velour* (velvet) and *crochet* (meaning 'little hook'). It was originally coined as a brand name, but has gradually become an everyday word for sticking things together. *Goodbye* is a much older and more complex blend – from 'God be with ye'.

For short

Some of our most common words are actually abbreviations. A *fax* is short for a facsimile, which is a word made from two morphemes: fac (meaning to make) and simile (as in *similar*). We can also see 'fac' in *factory*. *Soccer* is an abbreviation of the organising body 'Football

Association', specifically Assoc. This led to the slang reference 'socca' in 1889, which came to be written *soccer*.

Words that change their meaning over time

Nobody wants to be a *bully* these days, but back in the 1500s it meant sweetheart. In the 1700s a *jogger* was someone who moved 'heavily and dully'. *Cute* was an abbreviation of *acute* and in the 1700s meant sharp and quick-witted. It has since shifted meaning, but you can hear something of its original meaning in the expression 'Don't get cute with me'. And back in the 1700s a *go-cart* was a contraption for helping children learn to walk.

Not so obvious

Sometimes the morphemes in words are not so obvious. 'Carn' is from Latin for meat, and it is in *carnival*, originally the religious festival that marked the beginning of Lent and the giving up of meat. *Carnivore* is a compound of 'carni' and 'vore' (meaning eat, as in *voracious*). And *carnage* and *reincarnate* both have the 'carn' morpheme. It is even in *carnation*, a flower named for its flesh-coloured petals.

The famous battle site of *Gallipoli* is actually a compound of two Greek words: *kali* and *poli*. *Kali* means good or beautiful, and *poli* is city. We can see 'poli' in other words such as *politics, policy* and *metropolis*. *Kali* is in *kaleidoscope* meaning to look at beautiful things.

Most people know that to eavesdrop is to listen in on someone else's conversation. But the word was originally 'eavesdrip', referring to the water dripping off the eaves of a building. *Eavesdrop* came to describe the action of people standing within the eavesdrop area of a building, close enough to listen in on conversations inside the building. Perhaps they could then *gossip* about what they heard. *Gossip* has changed meanings over the centuries. It was originally a compound word: god + sibb (meaning a blood relation, as in sibling), and it was a word for a godparent. It then became used to describe a close friend, and eventually someone who engaged in idle talk.

Kidnap was originally 'kid nab', and came into more common usage from the 1600s, about the same time as slave traders began stealing people from Africa to work in the plantations of America.

Foolscap paper is named for the fool's cap (or jester's cap) that was the watermark for this size paper. And *midwife* is not actually the middle of a wife, as in midnight. *Mid* is the Old English word for 'with', so midwife means 'to be with the wife'.

Appendix 2

Common English morphemes

Prefixes	Meaning	Examples
To do with measurement		
bi-	twice	bicycle, biscuit (twice cooked)
di-	two	digraph, dioxide
en/em	intensify	enrage, encourage, empathy (em when followed by p and b)
hemi-	half	hemisphere
hex-	six	hexagon
hyper-	excess	hypertension, hyperactive
hypo-	below/under	hypoallergenic, hypothesis
mega-	big	megaphone, megabyte
micro-	small	microscope, microwave
mono-	one	monopoly, monotreme, monorail
milli-	thousand	millimetre, millipede
multi-	many	multiply, multimillionaire
octo-	eight	octopus, October
pent-	five	pentagon, pentathlon
poly-	many	polygon, polyglot
quad-	four	quadrangle, quadbike
semi-	half or part	semifinal, semicolon
super-	more than	superman, supernatural
tri-	three	triangle, tricycle, tripod
ultra-	extreme	ultramarathon, ultraviolet
uni-	one, singular	unicycle, unisex, uniform
To do with time		
fore-	before	forehead, foreword
meso-	middle	Mesozoic, Mesopotamia
mid-	middle	midday, midnight
neo-	new	neolithic, neonatal
paleo-	old	paleolithic, paleozoic
post-	after	postnatal, postmatch
pre-	before	prenatal, pregnant (pre – gnant = birth)
prim-	first	primary, primate
proto-	first	prototype, proton
re-	repeat	review, renovate (nova = new)

(cont.)

Prefixes	Meaning	Examples
To do with negation		
a or an	without/lacking	amoral, apathy, anarchy
anti-	opposite	antiseptic, anticlimax
contra-	against	contrary, contraband
counter-	against	counterclaim, counteract
de-	do the opposite of	decode, defrost
dis-	reverse	disrespect, disagree, dislike, display – disply = unfold
dys-	bad	dysfunctional, dyslexic
ex-	former/out	ex-wife, exclude (to keep out), exclaim (to cry out)
in, im, il, ir (dependent on the first letter of the following morpheme)	opposite – mostly used for multimorphemic words from Latin or French	in – describable in – decisive
im- for m, b and p		immobile, impossible
il- for l		illegal
ir- for r		irregular
mis-	wrong	mislead, mistake
non-	not	nonsense, nonverbal
pseudo-	fake	pseudonym, pseudoscience
un-	opposite – mostly used for short, single-morpheme base words	unhappy, unlock un – able (single morpheme) but in – ability (two morphemes) abil – ity
To do with location and movement		
a – from Old English	on	afloat, awash
ad-, ac- (dependent on the first letter of the following morpheme, ac for c)	towards	accommodation, advantage
be-	to make	bewitch, belittle
circum-	around	circumference, circumstance
co-, com-, con- depending upon the first letter of the following morpheme	together	cooperate, compete, correlate, collocate, confederate (federate = league), confuse (to fuse together so the parts are indistinguishable)
co- for vowels, h and g		
com- for p, b, m		
cor- for r		
col- for l		
con- for the rest		
epi-	upon	epicenter, epidermis (dermis = skin)
in-	in	internal, include
infra-	beneath	infrastructure, infrared
inter-	between	intermission, interrupt
intra-	inside	intravenous, introvert
omni-	everywhere	omnipresent, omnipotent

Prefixes	Meaning	Examples
pan-	everywhere, all-encompassing	panoramic, pandemic
para-	alongside	paramedic, parallel
peri-	around	periscope, perimeter
sub-	under	submarine, subtitle, subway

Suffixes	Meaning and function	Example
-able/-ible	Having the characteristic of x, likely to be x (x being the base word) Changes verbs or nouns to adjectives 'able' more commonly added to free morphemes 'ible' is more commonly added to bound morphemes	comfort – comfortable agree – agreeable horr-ible – (horr[or]) terr-ible – (terr[or]) in-cred-ible
-acy/-cy	Having the quality of x acy – Changes adjectives ending in ate to abstract nouns cy – changes adjectives ending in ant and ent to nouns	intricate – intricacy accurate – accuracy urgent – urgency pregnant – pregnancy
-age	The result of x Changes verbs to nouns	leak – leakage break – breakage
-age	A quantity of x Nouns to nouns	acre – acreage mile – mileage
-al	Having the property of x Changes nouns into adjectives	music – musical magic – magical
-al	The act of x Changes verbs into abstract nouns	survive – survival revive – revival
-an	Of or resembling x Changes nouns to adjectives	Australia – Australian reptile – reptilian
-ance, -ence	The act of x Changes verbs to abstract nouns	appear – appearance relevant – relevance differ – difference reside – residence
-ant, -ent	A person who does x Changes verbs to nouns	participate – participant celebrate – celebrant study – student preside – president
-ary	Is a part of x Nouns to adjectives	moment – momentary second – secondary
-ate	To cause x Verb ending	term (end) – terminate anim (life) – animate

(cont.)

Suffixes	Meaning and function	Example
-ate	Full of x Adjective ending Changes nouns into adjectives	passion – passionate fortune – fortunate
-ate	To have the characteristics of x Noun ending	prime – primate carbon – carbonate
-ation	Used with some verbs with no verb suffixes Changes verbs into abstract nouns	inform – information adapt – adaptation
-cation	Used with verbs ending with the verb suffix 'ify' Changes verbs to nouns	purify – purification classify – classification
-dom	State of being x Changes nouns to abstract nouns	wise – wisdom free – freedom
-ed	For adjectives – to be in a state of x Changes verbs to adjectives	interest – interested bore – bored
-ee	The person who participates in x Usually changes verbs into nouns	employ – employee train – trainee
-eer	Person who deals with x Noun to noun	mountain – mountaineer auction – auctioneer
-en	For verbs To become x Changes adjectives to verbs (verbs must be monosyllabic)	dark – darken cheap – cheapen
-en	For adjectives To have the characteristic of x Changes nouns to adjectives when the noun is monosyllabic	wood – wooden ash – ashen
-er	Person who does x Changes verbs into nouns	teach – teacher sing – singer
-ese	Belonging to x Changes nouns to adjectives	China – Chinese legal – legalese
-esque	Having the style of . . . Changes nouns into adjectives	statue – statuesque picture – picturesque
-ess	Female name for x Nouns to nouns	lion – lioness prince – princess
-ful	Full of x Changes nouns to adjectives State of being x	beauty – beautiful peace – peaceful

Suffixes	Meaning and function	Example
-hood	Changes nouns into abstract nouns	child – childhood neighbour – neighborhood
-ia	The condition of	dyslexia, insomnia
-ic	To have the characteristic of x Changes nouns into adjectives	romance – romantic metal – metallic
-ify	Cause to be x Adjectives into verbs Most often used with adjectives of one syllable and adjectives which end in a vowel sound	pure – purify glory – glorify
-ing	To extend x Changes verbs to nouns	meet – meeting gather – gathering
-ing	To have the characteristic of x Changes verbs to adjectives	bore – boring interest – interesting
-ion	State of x Changes verbs to nouns	act – action direct – direction
-ish	To become like x Changes nouns to adjectives	boy – boyish style – stylish
-ism	A system of beliefs related to x Noun to noun	race – racism age – ageism
-ist	Person connected with x Noun to noun	pyschiatr (healing the soul) – pyschiatrist dent (teeth) – dentist
-ity	To have the quality of x Changes adjectives to nouns	agile – agility fragile – fragility
-ise/-ize; NB: -ise preferred in Australian and British English; -ize preferred in US English	To cause to be x Changes adjectives or nouns to verbs Used with root words with more than one syllable, and which end in r, l, n, m, y	popular – popularise final – finalise victim – victimise memory – memorise
-ive	Characterised by x Changes verbs to adjectives	act – active persuade – persuasive
-less	Without x Changes nouns to adjectives	hope – hopeless fear – fearless
-let	A smaller version of x Noun to noun	pig – piglet drop – droplet

(cont.)

Suffixes	Meaning and function	Example
-ling	Related to x – sometimes offspring of x Noun to noun	earth – earthling duck – duckling
-like	Having the characteristic of x Nouns into adjectives (to describe the noun)	child – childlike gentleman – gentlemanlike
-ly	Having the characteristic of x Nouns into adjectives 'ly' began as a contraction of the suffix 'like'	friend – friendly love – lovely
-ly	Having the characteristic of x Adjectives into adverbs	quick – quickly angry – angrily
-ment	The act of doing x Changes verbs to abstract nouns	settle – settlement achieve – achievement
-ness	To have the condition of x Changes adjectives to abstract nouns	ill – illness happy – happiness
-oid	Having the shape of x Changes nouns to adjectives	andr (man) – Android tab (tablet) – tabloid
-ous	Full of x Changes nouns to adjectives	fame – famous venom – venomous
-proof	Keeps out x Changes nouns to adjectives	bullet – bulletproof water – waterproof
-ry	A broader description of x Nouns into broader nouns (occupations, places, collections)	dentist – dentistry baker – bakery
-ship	A relationship with x Changes concrete nouns into abstract nouns	friend – friendship partner – partnership
-some	Like/to have the characteristics of x Nouns to nouns	awe – awesome trouble – troublesome
-teen	Ten more than x	six – teen seven – teen
-th	State of x Changes adjectives to nouns	deep – depth strong – strength
-ty (a contraction of 'ten')	x multiplied by ten	six – ty seven – ty
-ty	To have the condition of x Changes adjectives to nouns	royal – royalty novel – novelty

Suffixes	Meaning and function	Example
-ward	In the direction of x	home – homeward
		south – southward
-y	Full of x	mist – misty
	Changes nouns to adjectives	rain – rainy
-y, -ie	Affectionate diminutive of x – usually applied to monosyllabic words	dog – doggy
		mum – mummy
		barbecue – barbie
	A particularly Australian trait is to reduce multisyllabic words to one syllable and then add the 'ie' or 'y'	football – footy
-y	In a state of x	jealous – jealousy
	Adjectives to nouns	honest – honesty

Base words	Meaning	Example
andr-	man/humankind	android, philander
anthrop-	human	philanthropy, anthropology
aqua-	water	aquarium, aquatic
arch-	chief/leader	monarchy, archbishop, architect
aster/astro-	star	astronaut, astronomy
atmos-	gas	atmosphere
aud-	hear	audio, audience
auto-	self	autograph, autobiography
bene/bon-	good	benefit, bonus
bio-	life	biology, biography
chron-	time	chronology, chronic, crony
crat-	rule	democrat, autocrat
cred-	believe/trust	credit, incredible
demo-	people	democrat, demographic
dict	speak words	predict, dictionary
dont/dent	teeth	dental, orthodontist
drome	road	aerodrome, dromedary
eco-	home	economics, ecology
fend	ward off	defend, fence
fin	end	finish, definite
-form	shape	transform, uniform
frac-	break	fraction, fracture
geo-	earth	geometry, geology
gno	to know	ignore, recognise
-gon	corner	pentagon, hexagon
grad-	step	grade, graduate, gradual
-graph	write	autograph, telegraph
happ	luck	happenstance, mishap
homo-	same	homophone, homosexual
hon-	worthy	honest, honour
hydr-	water	hydraulic, dehydrate

(cont.)

Base words	Meaning	Example
inter-	between	interview, interrupt
iatr	medical treatment	paediatric, psychiatrist
journ	day	journal, journey
kilo-	thousand	kilometre, kilobyte
lex	word	dyslexia, lexicon
lith-	stone	lithograph, lithosphere
-logy	study	biology, psychology
mal-	ill/wrong	malfunction, malady
mar-	sea	marine, submarine
metre	measure	metric, kilometre
nova	new	novice, renovate
nym, onoma	name	synonym, onomatopoeia
ortho-	correct/straight	orthography, orthodontist
pathy	feeling	sympathy, pathology
-pel	push	repel, expel
phil-	love	philosophy, philanthropy
-phobia	fear	hydrophobia, arachnophobia
-phon	voice/sound	telephone, symphony
phot-	light	photograph, photosynthesis
pod/ped	leg	centipede, podiatrist
polis-	city	police, politics
port	carry	porter, transport
psych-	spirit	psychology, psychiatrist
pus/pod	foot	octopus, podiatrist
quest	ask	request, question
-rupt	break	bankrupt, interrupt
-saur	lizard	dinosaur, brontosaurus
scope	look	telescope, periscope
spect	view/observe	spectator, inspect
-sphere	round	hemisphere, atmosphere
strat-	layer	stratosphere, strata
struct	build	structure, destruct
techno	craft/skill	technical, architect
tele-	over distance	television, telescope
thermo	heat	thermometer, geothermal
vis-	seeing	vision, vista
viv-	alive	vivid, revive
-volv	roll	revolve, evolve
zo	life	zoology, Mesozoic

Appendix 3

Ways into words

Some of the most frequently occurring words in English

Word	Phonology	Orthography	Morphology	Etymology
eight	eigh (long a) – t	A 'vowel' before 'igh' usually produces a long a sound, e.g. weight, freight, straight A consonant before 'igh' usually produces a long i sound e.g. light, fight		Originally written ehte pronounced with a hard 'h', as in the end of loch. With the arrival of the printing press, the use of 'gh' for this hard 'h' sound became standardised as evidenced in other words, e.g. fight, night
first	f – ir – st (consonant blend)	Note the use of the final consonant blend 'st' for use in representing the ordinal number first	A contraction of the compound word 'foremost'	The compound word foremost explains the meaning, as being the superlative; i.e. the most fore (fore = leading)
have	h – a – ve (silent)			Members of the verb family 'to have'. The ve, d, and s are endings on the base 'ha'. These endings indicate person and tense
has	h – a – d			
had	h – a – s (z)			
he	h – e (long ee sound)			Members of the family of personal pronouns
she	sh (digraph) – e (long ee sound)			
we	w – e (long ee sound)			
its (possessive)		No apostrophe Compare to other possessive pronouns, none of which use an apostrophe; e.g. we would never write his as hi's		Member of the family of possessive pronouns: mine, yours, his, hers, its, ours, theirs
know	kn – ow			Members of the verb family 'to know': know, knew, known
knew	kn – ew			The k was once pronounced. The original word for know was cnawan

little	l – i – tt – le	Double consonant after a short vowel	
make	m – a – ke ake is a common rime e.g bake, cake, fake, lake, take, wake, snake	Long vowel marked by silent e	The placement of a silent e on the end of the word to indicate when a word has a long vowel sound was a very early attempt by monk scribes to reform spelling, before the printing press and the dictionary
many	m – a (e) – n – y		Many has been spelled many ways, each reflecting the pronunciation of the users. Mony and meny were two common spellings. The southern English pronunciation of 'meny' has become predominant, while the spelling 'many' became the standard, reflecting the pronunciation in some dialects 'man – y'. This pronunciation is still evident in 'manifold'
one			Originally pronounced as in only, and still pronounced that way when we say: 'He is a good 'un.' Also evident in alone (all one) and atone (at one) Began to be pronounced 'won' in the thirteenth century in south-west England as a dialect difference. This current pronunciation is also evident in 'once'
only		A contraction of 'onelike' 'Like' is a suffix, as in childlike, that has contracted to become the suffix 'ly' e.g. friendly was once friendlike	Originally pronounced on – e – like

(cont.)

Word	Phonology	Orthography	Morphology	Etymology
or				Originally a contraction of 'other'
out	out			
about	a – b – ou – t		a – bout (originally meant on the outside of) The 'a' is the prefix we can see in afloat or awash 'bout' now changed in meaning; originally meant 'outside'	
people	p – eo – p – le			Originally spelled peeple until the spelling reforms of the sixteenth century when the spelling of many words was standardised to reflect the word's origins – in this case Norman French Related words have adopted the original Latin spelling of the root word popul, e.g. populous, population, popularity
said	s – ai – d		Morphemes of said, originally – say + ed. The spelling and pronunciation became sa – id, before the pronunciation shifted to 'sed'	Members of the verb family 'to say' Originally pronounced as 'sayed' as evidenced by earlier spellings 'sayde'
say	s – ay			
says	s – ay – s (z)	ay is a common rime e.g. play, may, day	Morphemes of 'says' = say + s. Often pronounced 'sez'	
these	th (non-aspirated) – e (long e) – se (z)			Members of the family of demonstrative pronouns
those	th (non-aspirated) – o (long o) – se (z)			
this	th (non-aspirated) – i – s			

they	th (non-aspirated) – ey (long 'a' sound)	Members of the family of pronouns that refer to third-person plural
them		The 'y', 'm' and 'ir' are endings on the same
their		base 'the'. These endings indicate the function of the pronoun
two		Originally pronounced as in twice. This is evident in other related words: between, twain, twin
		Twu was the original word when describing two male objects, and tu was the word for describing two neutral objects. Eventually the two words merged as English stopped using gender to describe nouns. 'Two' became the spelling and 'to' the pronunciation
use	u (y) – se (z) for the verb	
	u (y) – se (s) for the noun	
was	w – a (o) – s (z)	Members of the family of verbs – 'to be': am, is, are, was, were, been
is	i – s (z)	See the explanation of the 'wh' pattern in chapter 2
what	wh – a (o) – t	
when	wh – e – n	
why	wh – y (long i)	
which	wh – i – ch (digraph)	
who		Note that who has kept its pronunciation, beginning with an 'h' sound. It was once written hwo/hwa

(cont.)

Word	Phonology	Orthography	Morphology	Etymology
with	w – i – th (note: this may be the aspirated th or the non-aspirated th in that, depending on accent)			One of our oldest English words, originally meaning 'against'. This meaning is evident in 'withdraw' and 'withstand'
would should could	Onset and rime w – ould sh – ould c – ould			Members of the family of modal verbs, e.g.: will – would; shall – should; can – could See Appendix 1 for the history of these spellings
you your	y – ou (long oo sound) y – our (long or sound)		your = you + r	Members of the family of second-person pronouns: you, your, yours The second-person pronouns were once more differentiated. Second-person singular as the subject: you = thou Second-person singular as the object: you = thee Second-person plural as the subject: you = ye Second-person plural as the object: you = you

Some of the most frequently used words in children's writing

Word	Phonology	Orthography	Morphology	Etymology
against	a – g – ai – n – st		Base word – gain a – gain – st	Original meaning of gain was opposite of. This has now been mostly lost, but evident in 'gainsay'
another			an – other	See entry for 'or'
asked	a – sk		ask – ed	Originally written and pronounced as 'ax' and still often heard pronounced this way
beautiful		Adding suffixes to base words ending with the consonant 'y' pattern – change the 'y' to 'i'	beauty + ful (adjective suffix)	French origin word explains the eau pattern. Beau is French for beautiful
because	b – e – c – au – se (z)		be – cause, originally from 'by this cause'	
birthday	b – ir – th (aspirated)		birth – day	Originally two words, then hyphenated, joined in the 1700s
called	c – all NB: the common rime pattern 'all', e.g. ball, fall, small Morpheme 'ed' sounds like 'd' in words ending with phonemes: l, r, b, g, v, z, m, n, ng, th (non-aspirated) and vowels		call – ed (marking the past tense)	
coming	c – o – me	Drop the e on the end of words when adding suffixes	come – ing	The spelling cum was frequent, but scribes began to replace 'u' with 'o' before the letters m, n and u. This was done because the downstrokes of the calligraphic 'u' made it difficult to see where one letter ended and *(cont.)*

Word	Phonology	Orthography	Morphology	Etymology
				another started. This is responsible for the 'o' in a number of common words that were originally spelled with a phonetic 'u' e.g. some, son, tongue, love
didn't		This apostrophe replaces the 'o' in 'not' in the contraction of two words	compound of 'did' and 'not'	
different		differ. Double the consonant after short vowel	differ – ent (adjective suffix)	
evening			even – ing (suffix for nouns, e.g. blessing)	The modern word 'eve' was originally 'even'. The 'en' sound was dropped on some words over time, e.g. maiden became maid
every			ever – y	Originally a contraction of 'ever' and 'each'
favourite		US spelling is favorite. Webster shifted many 'our' spellings to 'or' in his 1806 dictionary, e.g. colour – color. English spelling retained 'our'	favour + ite (adjective suffix)	
finally			final + ly (adverb suffix)	Final from finale – Italian for last movement in music or performance
friend	fr (consonant blend) – ie – nd (consonant blend)			The two vowels were once pronounced 'fri – end'. Pronunciation has changed; spelling remains the same. See entry for 'reality'
going	g – o – i – ng		go – ing	'ing' makes the present continuous tense in this verb

Word	Rule	Morpheme/Suffix	Explanation
happy	double consonant after short vowel	happ + y (adjective suffix)	Happ is an old word for luck, evident in modern words, e.g. perhaps, mishap
heard h – ear – d		hear – ed	From the verb family 'to hear': hear, hears, heard
lived l – i – ve NB: short i despite the silent e. Also as in give	Drop the e on the end of words when adding suffixes	live – ed	The 'ed' on lived could mark the past tense: I once lived in New York, or could mark an adjective: My lived experience Scribes tended not to double 'v's after short vowels because it then looked like 'w'
looked l – oo – k ook – a common rime, e.g. book, cook, took Morpheme 'ed' sounds like 't' in words ending with phonemes: p, k, f, s, sh, ch, th (aspirated)		look – ed (past tense suffix)	
morning		morn – ing (suffix for nouns, e.g. blessing)	morn is related to morrow, as in 'tomorrow'
night n – igh (long i) – t			gh once pronounced; see 'eight'
played pl (consonant blend) – ay (long a) ay common rime; see 'say'	Usually when adding suffixes to words ending in 'y', we change the 'y' to 'i', except if the 'y' is preceded by a vowel, as in played	play – ed (past tense suffix)	
really r – ea (long e) – l		real – ly (adverb suffix)	The two vowels were once pronounced 're – al'. This pronunciation is still evident in 'reality'. Many vowel digraphs in English words today were once pronounced as two vowel phonemes, e.g. bread

(cont.)

Word	Phonology	Orthography	Morphology	Etymology
Saturday Sunday			Satur – day Sun – day	Saturday named after the Roman god Saturn Sun – day Moon – day (Mon day)
school	s – ch – oo – l			See chapter 2
something	s – ome making 'um' see the entry for 'coming'		some – thing some day, some one, some how, some where, some time, some body etc	Written as two separate words until the 1600s
stopped	st – o – p op is a common rime: hop, flop, shop	Doubling consonants after short vowels when adding suffixes	stop – ed	
suddenly		Double consonant after short vowel	sudden – ly (adverb suffix)	originally sudden – like. See entry for 'only'
teacher	t – ea – ch		teach – er (noun suffix)	Teacher is an Old English word, meaning to show or point out
thought	th – ough – t ought common rime: bought, fought, brought			gh once pronounced; see entry for 'eight'
tried		When adding suffixes to words ending with a 'consonant y', change the 'y' to 'i'	try – ed	Related to trial, and to try someone in court, and a football try, which was a 'try at goal'

Some of the 'common' words identified by the Australian National Assessment program (NAPLAN)

Word	Phonology	Orthography	Morphology	Etymology
action			act – ion (noun suffix)	
angry			anger – y (adjective suffix) Also hunger – y	The 'e' was dropped to reflect pronunciation
believe				Was spelled beleeve. Probably changed at the time of first dictionary writing to be similar to relieve
climb	cl – i – mb			'b' originally pronounced. From the Old English word climban. 'b' still pronounced in related word clamber
couple	c – ou – ple			French – originally just for a married couple but now for any two things in English
delight	l – igh – t common rime 'ight', e.g fight, might, night			Spelled delite until the sixteenth century when it changed under influence of light, flight, etc.
disagree			dis – agree	a – gree Gree obsolete English word meaning pleasure or goodwill. This meaning still evident in some usage of the word agreeable Gre is a modern French word meaning liking, desire
fruit	fr – ui – t		Exists as a morpheme in fruitful, fruitless or when something comes to fruition	French origin, which explains the uit pattern. The two vowels were once pronounced. Note that 'fruit – ion' shows the original pronunciation of the two vowels Originally in English, meaning all agricultural products and any profit from that produce (as in the 'fruits of my labour')

(cont.)

Word	Phonology	Orthography	Morphology	Etymology
happiness		Change y to i when adding a suffix	happy – ness (abstract noun suffix)	See entry for 'happy' for history
holiday		Change y to i when adding a suffix	Holy – day	The fish 'halibut' has the same root: hali = holy; butt = flat fish
involve	l –au – gh		in – volve (base word meaning roll) re – volve: roll again	Car brand Volvo has taken its name from this Latin base word
laugh				An onomatopoeic word
length	l – e – ng (digraph) – th (digraph) t – ake Common rime pattern		long – th (noun suffix)	Originally with a 'hard' – gh – sound, as in Scottish loch
mistake		Long vowel marked by the silent e	mis (negation prefix) – take	Pronunciation changed from 'o' to 'e'
money	m – o – n – ey			Named for the Roman goddess of prosperity, Moneta. Coins were produced near her temple – hence also the root for 'mint'
movie	m – o – v – ie			An abbreviation of 'moving pictures'
phone	ph – o – ne	Long vowel marked by the silent e	Tele + phone	Abbreviation of 'telephone' 'ph' indicates words originally from Greek
question	qu – e – st (consonant blend) est is a common rime, e.g. west, best, nest	NB: qu always appear together except in recent foreign import words, e.g. Qatar, and acronyms, e.g. Qantas	quest – ion (noun suffix)	'qu' was originally written 'cw' in Old English words, e.g. queen was cwen The shift to qu came with the Norman occupation of England and the subsequent application of French letter patterns to existing English words

quiet	qu – ie (diphthong) – t Note the gliding vowel, which differentiates this word phonologically from 'quite'	See 'question'	Quiet is from the same Latin root as 'requiem' in which the two distinct vowel sounds are more easily heard
safety	s – a – fe – t – y	safe + ty	
sign		long a vowel with e silent 'g'	Sign is from the Latin, meaning to make a mark. You can hear the g in signal, signature, insignia
window			Originally a compound word: wind eye, describing an unglazed hole in a roof. This was a word brought into English by the Vikings. The Old English word was eyethirl, which meant eyehole

Some of the most frequently misspelled words in English

Word	Phonology	Orthography	Morphology	Etymology
accommodation			The morphemes explain the double letters ac = to com = combine mode = to make suitable ate = verb suffix	
achieve			a – chieve a = to chieve = lead, succeed	Chieve is an obsolete spelling of 'chief'. 'Chef' is another version of this word
argument		Drop the final 'e' when adding a suffix	argue – ment	
definitely			definite – ly	From define, which is from the Latin roots: de = to; fine = finish In other related words 'definitive' and 'finite', it is easier to hear the vowel sounds for the letter 'i'
language			langue – age langue = now obsolete, meant style of expression age = noun suffix	Langue comes from the Latin lingua, meaning 'language' or 'tongue' The term lingo comes from this root, as do such words as bilingual and linguistics
misspell		Double the consonant after a short vowel	mis (negating prefix) + spell	Spell is derived from an Old English word meaning to tell a story – gospel is a contraction of the compound 'good spell', meaning good tidings, or good story

separate	Double the consonant after the short vowel	se – par – ate se = apart par = to make ready ate = verb/adjective suffix	par is the same Latin root used for 'prepare' and 'parent', which may help remember the first 'a' in separate
tomorrow	Originally written as two words, then hyphenated, before becoming one word in the 1960s	to – morrow	See entry for morning The expression was originally 'to morn' and the 'n' was eventually dropped to become 'to mor'. Various dialects began to put an 'o' on the end, leading to the current spelling
unnecessary		The morphemes help explain the double 'n' un – ne – cess – ary It is a double negative word. Necessary means 'not avoidable' ne = not cess = stop ary = adjective suffix	

Appendix 4

Spelling Scope and Sequence

	Kindergarten			
Morphology	Phonology/graphology	Orthography	Etymology	Visual
Recognise and understand the morphemes in compound words where the base words are common and the pronunciation of the base words remains the same in the compound word: e.g. football, Sunday	Know that spoken sounds and words can be written down using letters of the alphabet, e.g. attempting to 'sound out' words as they write	Recognise lower case and upper case letters as different representations of the same letter	Recognise words come from other languages in common and familiar words, e.g. pizza	Know how to write some high-frequency sight words and known words that may not be phonically regular, e.g. of, the, have
Recognise and know how to use inflectional **suffixes** that mark tense, e.g. play – ed and play – ing	Use the most common single graphemes for consonant sounds in the initial, medial and final positions of the word	Recognise and use the letters of the alphabet to represent sounds and meaning	Recognise words can come from people's names (eponyms), e.g. pavlova	
Recognise and know how to use inflectional **suffixes** that mark plurals – with 's', e.g. dog – s and cat – s	Use the most common single graphemes for short vowel sounds, e.g. h – a – t, m – u – m		Recognise words can represent sounds (onomatopoeia), e.g. moo, meow	
Recognise and know how to use inflectional **suffixes** that mark the third person – with 's', e.g. she play – s, she run – s	Recognise and use onset and phonically regular rime patterns to spell words with the same rime pattern, e.g. c – at, h – at			
Recognise and know how to use derivational **prefixes** with an obvious meaning and which do not change the pronunciation or spelling of the base word, e.g. un – happy	Recognise and use phonically regular one-syllable words, e.g. in, on, had			
Recognise and know how to use derivational **suffixes** with an obvious meaning and which do not change the pronunciation or spelling of the base word, e.g. ful				

Morphology	Phonology/graphology	Orthography	Etymology	Visual
Recognise and understand the morphemes in less obvious but commonly used compound words where the pronunciation of the base word remains the same, e.g. grandmother, afternoon, username	Recognise and use common long vowel patterns, e.g. w – e; f – ee – t; m – a – t – e	Recognise and use capital letters to signal proper nouns	Recognise and use words that come from other languages in words they read in books, e.g. kangaroo (Australian Indigenous language) and words they use in all curriculum areas, e.g. tri-angle (Greek – three corners)	Use visual memory to check phonically irregular words
Recognise and know how to use inflectional **suffixes** that mark tense, and change the spelling of the base word, e.g. hop – hopped, hopping	Recognise and use onset and more complex phonically regular rime patterns, to spell words with the same rime pattern, e.g. l – ate, m – ate, h – ate	Understand when to use 'es' for plurals when the word ends with s, sh, ch, z, x, f; e.g. witches, buses	Understand why words are not spelled the way they sound because of the history of English – focus on etymological stories for commonly used words, e.g. what, why, where	
Recognise and know how to use inflectional **suffixes** that mark plurals – with 'es', e.g. witch – es, box – es	Recognise and use the common consonant digraphs, e.g. sh, th, ch, ck	Understand when to double the final consonant when adding a suffix to a base word with a short vowel, e.g. hit – hitting, hop – hopping	Recognise words can come from people's names (eponyms), e.g. lamington, sandwich	
Recognise and know how to use inflectional **suffixes** that mark the third person – with 'es', e.g. she go – es, she do – es	Recognise and use the consonant blends, e.g. bl, fl, gl, tr, br	Understand the double letters in some single morphemes can be explained by the preceding short vowel, e.g. little, dribble	Recognise words can represent sounds (onomatopoeia), e.g. zip, whiz	
Recognise and know how to use inflectional suffixes that mark the comparative with 'er' and 'est' and do not change the	Recognise and use the most common vowel digraphs, e.g. ea, ou, oo		Recognise words can be made by combining parts of other words (portmanteaus), e.g. brunch	
	Recognise and use phonically regular one-syllable words containing common letter clusters including digraphs and blends, e.g. from, with		Recognise words can be made	
	Recognise and use the silent e on the end of common words, e.g. mat – mate			

(cont.)

	Year 1		
Morphology	Phonology/graphology	Orthography	Etymology	Visual
spelling of the base word, e.g. small – er, small – est	Recognise and use common silent letters at the beginning of words with an etymological explanation, e.g. what, why		from abbreviations and acronyms, e.g. ANZAC, (omni)bus
Recognise and know how to use derivational **prefixes** with an obvious meaning and which do not change the spelling of the base word, e.g. re – use, super – man			
Recognise and know how to use derivational **suffixes** with an obvious meaning and which do not change the spelling of the base word, e.g. child – like			
Recognise and know how to use very common derivational **suffixes** with less obvious meanings and which do not change the spelling of the base word, e.g. teach – er, six – teen, mist – y			

	Year 2			
Morphology	Phonology/graphology	Orthography	Etymology	Visual
Recognise and understand the morphemes in compound words where the pronunciation of the base words changes, e.g. breakfast, forehead, cupboard	Recognise and use onset and rime patterns to spell words with the same rime pattern, e.g. l – ight, m – ight	Recognise and use capital letters to signal acronyms, e.g. UK	Recognise and use words that come from other languages in words they read in books, e.g. robot (Czech), and use in other curriculum areas, e.g. octa – gon (Greek)	Use visual memory to check phonically irregular words
		Understand when to drop the 'e' from the base word when adding a suffix that begins with a vowel, e.g. care – caring; care – careful		
Recognise and understand the morphemes in common contracted words, e.g. didn't, doesn't	Recognise and use the consonant trigraphs, e.g. tch	Understand how to add suffixes to words ending in 'y'	Understand why words are not spelled the way they sound because of the history of English – focus on the Norman invasions and the growth of the English vocabulary. The difference between Old English words and French origin words, e.g. pig/pork	
	Recognise and use the vowel/ consonant trigraph 'igh' understanding when it is preceded by a consonant it makes a long 'i' sound, e.g. might, light	If the word ends with a 'consonant y' pattern – change the y to i before adding the suffix, e.g. fry – fried		
Recognise and know how to use inflectional morphemes that mark the comparative with 'er' and 'est' and which change the spelling of the base word, e.g. funny – funnier, funniest	When it is preceded by a vowel, it makes a long 'a' sound, e.g. eight, straight	If the suffix begins with 'i', don't change the base word, e.g. fry – frying		
Recognise and know how to use commonly used **derivational prefixes** with less obvious meanings, e.g.	Recognise and use the consonant digraph blends, e.g. thr, shr	If the word ends with a 'vowel y' pattern – do not change the y before adding a suffix, e.g. monkey – monkeys, monkeying	Understand that some letter patterns in English are explained by their etymology, e.g. ph – phone, cy – cycle (Greek graphemes)	

(cont.)

| | Year 2 | | | |
Morphology	Phonology/graphology	Orthography	Etymology	Visual
micro – microscope, octo – octopus, dis – disagree	Recognise and use diphthongs, e.g. boy, now		Recognise words can come from people's names or places (eponyms), e.g. panic, biro	
Recognise and know how to use **derivational suffixes** with less obvious meanings but which are commonly used, e.g. wood – en, child – ish	Recognise and use less transparent graphemes with etymological explanations, e.g. sch – ool, ph – one		Recognise words can represent sounds (onomatopoeia), e.g. splash, shriek	
Recognise and understand homophones where the morphemes in the words explain the spelling difference, e.g. aloud – allowed (allow – ed); its – it's (it is)	Recognise and use common silent letters at the beginning of words with an etymological explanation, e.g. know, knee		Recognise words can be made by combining parts of other words (portmanteaus), e.g. motel	
			Recognise words can be made from abbreviations and acronyms, e.g. ANZAC, pants (pantaloons)	

Morphology	Phonology/graphology	Orthography	Etymology	Visual
	Recognise and use less common graphemes with etymological explanations, e.g. magic, beauty	Understand how the grammatical category of possessives is signalled through apostrophes and how to use apostrophes with common nouns	Recognise and do some independent investigation of words which come from other languages in words they read in books, e.g. titan, and use in other curriculum areas, e.g. semicircle	Use visual memory to check phonically irregular words
	Recognise and use common silent letters at the end of words with an etymological explanation, e.g. lamb, comb	Understand when to use 'i' before 'e' except after 'c' in words where there is a long 'e' sound, e.g. believe, receive. Exception: seize	Understand why words are not spelled the way they sound because of the history of English – focus on the arts and sciences and the growth of the English vocabulary through Latin and Greek, e.g. telephone	
			Understand that some letter patterns in English are explained by their etymology, e.g. ch (Greek) – Christmas, chord; et (French) – ballet, crochet	
Recognise and understand the morphemes in compound words where the pronunciation of the base words changes, e.g. breakfast, forehead, cupboard			Recognise words can come from people's names or places (eponyms), e.g. titan, Queensland (named for Queen Victoria)	
Recognise and understand the morphemes in more challenging contracted words, e.g. wouldn't, could've, won't			Recognise words can represent sounds (onomatopoeia), e.g. splash, shriek	
Recognise and know how to use derivational **prefixes** with a more obvious meaning but which are less commonly used, e.g. semi – semifinal, semicircle; neo – neonatal			Recognise words can be made by combining parts of other words (portmanteaus), e.g. splurge	
Recognise and know how to use derivational **prefixes** with less obvious meanings, e.g. de – decode, in – incredible			Recognise words can be made from abbreviations and acronyms, e.g. radar and fridge	
Recognise and know how to use common derivational **suffixes** that change the pronunciation of the base word, e.g. comfort – able; differ – ent, act – ion				
Recognise and know how to use common derivational **suffixes** that change the spelling of the base word, e.g. fortunate – fortune – ate; glorious – glory – ous				

Year 4				
Morphology	Phonology/graphology	Orthography	Etymology	Visual
Recognise and understand the morphemes in compound words where the morphemes are less commonly used alone, e.g. cornmeal, wardrobe, forefront Recognise and know how to use less common derivational **prefixes** with less obvious meanings, e.g. hyper – active; in – effective Recognise and know how to use derivational **suffixes** that change the spelling and pronunciation of the base word, e.g. agility – agile – ity; Chinese – China – ese	Recognise and use less common graphemes with etymological explanations, e.g. kayak, emoji Recognise and use silent letters in the middle of words with an etymological explanation, e.g. ghost	Understand how the grammatical category of possessives is signalled through apostrophes and how to use apostrophes with collective nouns, e.g. children's writing and plurals, e.g. students' writing	Recognise and do some independent investigation of words that come from other languages in words they read in books, e.g. kaleidoscope, and use in other curriculum areas, e.g. perimeter Understand why words are not spelled the way they sound because of the history of English – focus on trade expansion, e.g. catamaran, kizmet Understand that some letter patterns in English are explained by their etymology, e.g. kayak (Inuit), unique (French) Recognise words can come from people's names or places (eponyms), e.g. macadamia Recognise words can represent sounds (onomatopoeia), e.g. whisper, sneeze Recognise words can be made by combining parts of other words (portmanteaus), e.g. chortle Recognise words can be made from abbreviations, e.g. scuba, movies	Use visual memory to check phonically irregular words

Morphology	Phonology/graphology	Orthography	Etymology	Visual
Recognise and understand the morphemes in less used compound words with more unusual morphemes, e.g. happenstance, manifold, gainsay	Recognise and use less common graphemes with etymological explanations, e.g. queue	Recognise and represent uncommon plurals, e.g. foci	Understand that the pronunciation, spelling and meanings of words have histories and change over time, and this explains some apparently irregular spelling patterns, e.g. yacht	Use visual memory to check phonically irregular words
Recognise and know how to use derivational **prefixes** that change according to the initial letters of the base word, e.g. im – possible; il – legal; ir – resistible	Recognise and use less common silent letters in the middle of words with an etymological explanation, e.g. debt	Understand how the grammatical category of possessives is signalled through apostrophes and how to use apostrophes with proper nouns ending with s, e.g. Chris' writing	Understand why words are not spelled the way they sound because of the history of English – focus on language change and differences between varieties of English, e.g. color, colour	
Recognise and know how to use derivational suffixes that are additional to a word with an existing suffix, e.g. 'cation'; purification: pure + ify + cation; 'ation' victimisation: victim – ise – ation	Understand that different social and geographical dialects or accents exist in English		Understand that some unusual letter patterns in English are explained by their etymology, e.g. psy – psychology; pn – pneumonia	
			Recognise and use and independently investigate words that come from other languages in words they read in their own environment, e.g. bluetooth, and use in other curriculum areas, e.g. photosynthesis	
Recognise and know how to use less common derivational suffixes, e.g. statuesque – statue – esque; employee – employ – ee			Recognise words can come from people's names or places (eponyms), e.g. joule, watt	
			Recognise words can represent sounds (onomatopoeia), e.g. laugh, cough	
			Recognise words can be made by combining parts of other words (portmanteaus), e.g. modem, Brangelina	
			Recognise words can be made from abbreviations, e.g. taser, sonar, camera	

References

Adoniou, M. 2014. 'What should teachers know about spelling?', *Literacy* 48(3): 144–54

Apel, K. 2014. 'A comprehensive definition of morphological awareness: Implications for assessment.' *Topics in Language Disorders* 34(3): 197–209

Apel, K., J. Masterson & P. Hart. 2004. *Integration of Language Components in Spelling: Language and Literacy Learning in Schools*. Ed. E. Silliman & P. Wilkinson. New York: Guildford Press: 292–315

Apel, K., J. Masterson & N. Niessen. 2004. 'Spelling assessment frameworks.' *Handbook of Language and Literacy Development and Disorders*. Ed. C. Stone, E. Silliman, B. Ehren & K. Apel. New York: Guildford Press: 644–60

Apel, K., D. Brimo, E. Diehm & L. Apel. 2013. 'Morphological awareness intervention with kindergartners and first and second grade students from low socioeconomic status homes: A feasibility study.' *Language, Speech and Hearing Services in Schools* 44(April): 161–73

Arndt, E. & B. Foorman. 2010. 'Second graders as spellers: What types of errors are they making?' *Assessment for Effective Intervention* 36: 57–67

Australian Curriculum, Assessment and Reporting Authority. 2013. 'Spelling Reference List.' *NAPLAN 2013 Persuasive Writing Marking Guide*. Sydney: ACARA, 98–103 <www.nap.edu.au>

Bailet, L. 2004. 'Spelling instructional and intervention frameworks.' *Handbook of Language and Literacy Development and Disorders*. Ed. C. Stone, E. Silliman, B. Ehren & K. Apel. New York: Guildford Press, 661–78

Berninger, V., R. Abbott, W. Nagy & J. Carlisle. 2010. 'Growth in phonological, orthographic and morphological awareness in Grades 1 to 6.' *Journal of Psycholinguistic Research* 39: 141–63

Boynton Hauerwas, L. & J. Walker. 2004. 'What can children's spelling of running and jumped tell us about their need for spelling instruction?' *Reading Teacher* 58(2): 168–76

Bryant, P., T. Nunes & R. Barros. 2014. 'The connection between children's knowledge and use of grapho-phonic and morphemic units in written text and their learning at school.' *British Journal of Educational Psychology* 84: 211–25

Carlisle, J. 2010. 'Effects of instruction in morphological awareness on literacy achievement: An integrative review.' *Reading Research Quarterly* 45(4): 464–87

Cobb, T. & B. Laufer. 2021. 'The nuclear word family list: A list of the most frequent family members, including base and affixed words.' *Language Learning.* <https://doi.org/10.1111/lang.12452>

Daffern, T. 2015. 'The development of a spelling assessment tool informed by Triple Word Form theory.' *Australian Journal of Language and Literacy* 38(2): 72–82

Department for Education. 2014. 'English Appendix 1 Spelling.' *National Curriculum in England: English Programmes of Study.* <https://www.gov.uk/government/publications/national-curriculum-in-england-english-programmes-of-study>

Goodwin, A. & S. Ahn. 2010. 'A meta-analysis of morphological interventions: Effects on literacy achievement of children with literacy difficulties.' *Annals of Dyslexia* 60: 183–208

Graham, S., P. Morphy, K.R. Harris, B. Fink-Chorzempa, B. Saddler, S. Moran, L. Mason. 2008. 'Teaching spelling in the primary grades: A national survey of instructional practices and adaptations.' *American Educational Research Journal* 4(3): 796–825

Graham, S. & T. Santangelo. 2014. 'Does spelling instruction make students better spellers, readers and writers? A meta-analytic review.' *Reading and Writing* 27: 1703–43

Henry, M. 1989. 'Children's word structure knowledge: Implications for decoding and spelling instruction.' *Reading and Writing: An Interdisciplinary Journal* 2: 135–52

Hilte, M. & P. Reitsma. 2011. 'Activating the meaning of a word facilitates the integration of orthography: Evidence from spelling exercises in beginning spellers.' *Journal of Research in Reading* 34(3): 333–45

Johnston, F. 2001. 'Exploring classroom teachers' spelling practices and beliefs.' *Reading Research and Instruction* 40(2): 143–56

Kessler, B. & R. Treiman. 2003. 'Is English spelling chaotic? Misconceptions concerning its irregularity.' *Reading Psychology* 24: 267–89

Kim, Y.S., K. Apel & S. Al Otaiba. 2013. 'The relation of linguistic awareness and vocabulary to word reading and spelling for first-grade students participating in response to intervention.' *Language, Speech and Hearing Services in Schools* 44: 337–47

Kohnen, S., L. Nickels & A. Castles. 2009. 'Assessing spelling skills and strategies: A critique of available resources.' *Australian Journal of Learning Difficulties* 14(1): 113–50

Kohnen, S., L. Nickels & M. Coltheart. 2010. 'Skill generalisation in teaching spelling to children with learning difficulties.' *Australian Journal of Learning Difficulties* 15(2): 115–29

Levesque, K.C., H. Breadmore & S.H. Deacon. 2021. 'How morphology impacts reading and spelling: advancing the role of morphology in models of literacy development.' *Journal of Research in Reading* 44(1): 10–26

Mitchell, A. & S. Brady. 2014. 'Assessing affix knowledge using both psuedoword and real-word measures.' *Topics in Language Disorders* 34(3): 210–27

O'Sullivan, O. 2000. 'Understanding spelling.' *Reading* 34(1): 9–16

Pittas, E. & T. Nunes. 2014. 'The relation between morphological awareness and reading and spelling in Greek: A longitudinal study.' *Reading and Writing* 27: 1507–27

Siegel, L. 2008. 'Morphological awareness skills of English language learners and children with dyslexia.' *Topics in Language Disorders* 28(1): 15–27

Treiman, R. & D. Bourassa. 2000. 'The development of spelling skill.' *Topics in Language Disorders* (May): 1–18

Index